Walks in The Mysterious Yorkshire Dales

Graham Dugdale

Published by Sigma Leisure – an imprint of
Sigma Press, 1 South Oak Lane, Wilmslow, Cheshire SK9 6AR, England.

British Library Cataloguing in Publication Data
A CIP record for this book is available from the British Library.

ISBN: 1-85058-730-2

Typesetting and Design by: Sigma Press, Wilmslow, Cheshire.

Cover photograph: The Strid on the River Wharfe (Graham Dugdale)

Maps and photographs: Graham Dugdale

Printed by: MFP Design and Print

Disclaimer: the information in this book is given in good faith and is believed to be correct at the time of publication. No responsibility is accepted by either the author or publisher for errors or omissions, or for any loss or injury howsoever caused. Only you can judge your own fitness, competence and experience.

Prologue

What can't be explained by History
Will likely pertain to Mystery
When imagination takes the Wheel
Of Life, and all we think and feel.

By its very nature, a mystery encompasses a host of perplexing and obscure connotations, that tantalising brew of strange, odd, sometimes
even bizarre events that lack any formal definition or coherence. Yet mysteries alone are perfectly capable of solution as the great detective Sherlock
Holmes proved on more than one occasion.

The same is so with many of the 'mysteries' contained within this volume, where you the reader will, in due course, become an active partici-
pant by unravelling a series of clues and discovering that truth may indeed
be stranger than fiction. It cannot be denied that the converse is also an accurate depiction of some of the mysteries on offer.

These conundrums often form an essential chapter embracing our past
heritage, even though the chief participants along with their hardware in
the form of buildings have long since dissolved into the landscape. Such is
the mystery surrounding our detective hero's creator, the legendary Arthur
Conan Doyle and his family connections at Masongill near Ingleton. And
even the transit of the dead along the Old Corpse Road between Keld and
Grinton in Swaledale raises questions. Whether or not certain bodies were
mixed up following a 'rest' at one of the numerous taverns along the route is
open to debate. Such stories were often handed down by word of mouth
over a flagon or two during long winter nights and cannot be substantiated.

Mystical tales have long held a mesmerising fascination for visitors to
the Dales. And doubtless the arrival of carriages from distant parts back in
the late 18th century encouraged locals to exaggerate the otherwise mun-
dane into grandiose exploits. Held spellbound beneath flickering candlelight by the eloquent rendition concerning the Giant of Penhill, tourists
were more than willing to slake local thirsts at the Wensleydale Heifer in
West Witton in exchange for a magnetic evening of ghostly entertainment.
These new arrivals began to invade the previously isolated valleys of Yorkshire and loved nothing more than to be scared out of their wits by mythical
tales of haunted houses, nebulous apparitions and disappearing villages –
safely in the comfort of a warm hostelry of course.

In those distant times when fairies, boggles and phantoms were not to be
dismissed out of hand, the myths and legends of the Dales often contained
some semblance of truth, albeit secured by a gossamer thread. But at what

point do reality and fantasy diverge along differing trails? That is the question frequently asked but never satisfactorily answered. If it were, this entire fascination with all things mysterious would evaporate like Father Christmas to a growing child. And that would never do, now would it?

So enjoy flirting with the spirit of Emily Norton at Rylstone; speculate by all means as to the feasibility of Will Nevison's wicked leap over Gordale Scar; and mingle with the ghostly navvies at Ribblehead. But most of all enjoy the fine selection of outstanding walks on offer amidst the wild and romantic setting that is the Yorkshire Dales.

The Walks

In marked contrast to the scalloped moulding of England's craggy 'rooftop', the Dales of Yorkshire are initially less dramatic in appearance. Especially when viewed from the air, green waves of rolling moorland chopped up with deep river valleys give the impression of a wild and barren terrain that has little to offer the fell wanderer who relishes the solid feel of hard rock beneath his boots.

As you will soon discover, nothing could be further from the truth. From the monumental gash that is Gordale Scar to the startling profile of Ingleborough's trenchant snout, the topography that typifies the limestone dales exudes a degree of individuality that grabs our attention, refusing to let go. The subdued terrain of the upland moors might lack the histrionic impact of Malham Cove, but these lonely tracts with only the indigenous sheep for company are what hill walking is all about.

Mysterious occurrences do, however, invariably stick close to the more settled localities, ensuring that most of the walks on offer keep to the lower slopes of valleys. Only two venture above the magical 2000ft contour that automatically confers mountain status. And even then, the starting points are quite high.

All the walks take advantage of existing footpaths along rights of way noted on the appropriate Ordnance Survey map in green. In my opinion, there is no pleasure to be gained from drunkenly blundering across featureless belts of ankle-jarring, tussocky moor so such meanderings are kept to a bare minimum. Many of the wide open spaces are thankfully traversed by means of rough, walled drove roads established over the centuries for the movement of cattle herds to market.

As the vast majority of visitors to the Dales are more than likely to use a car, the walks have been arranged in the customary circular manner, starting and finishing at the same place. In these times of ever-decreasing rural public transport, the use of a private vehicle must be regarded as a necessity. Indeed, many of the remote valleys are way off the beaten track and could not otherwise be visited.

Key to Maps

A6 Main Roads	Limestone Pavements
B 5270 Secondary Roads	▲ Summits & Cairns
Minor Roads	310 Spot Heights
Railways	Main Walls
Main rights-of-way	Main Fences
Route to follow	Hedging
Rivers & Streams	P Parking for Cars
Lakes & Tarns	Buildings
Marshy Ground	Bridges
Coniferous Woods	+ Churches
Deciduous Woods	G Gates
Mixed Woodland	S Stiles
Steep Crags	FB Footbridges

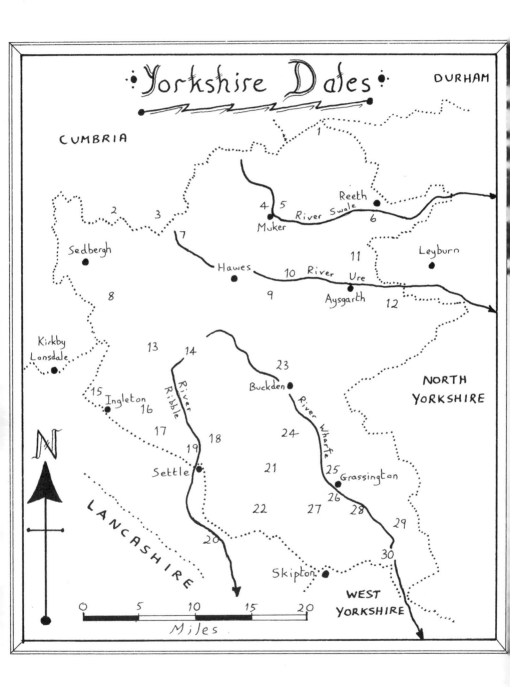

Contents

1. Tan Hill

Gun but Not Forgotten

Mystery: The Pistol-packin' Publican, GR 897067

Distance Walked: 8½ miles

Total Height Climbed: 350 feet, 107 metres

Start/Finish: Ample parking space is available in the vicinity of the Tan Hill Inn.

Terrain: Wild, featureless moorland swathed in heather appears to roll on forever, with no prominent landmarks.

Nearest Shops: None within easy reach so make use of the facilities offered by the Tan Hill Inn.

Map Required: Ordnance Survey 1:25000 Outdoor Leisure 30, Yorkshire Dales Northern & Central areas

The high Pennine moors must rank as some of the harshest, most inhospitable terrain in the country. Yet on a fine day with sunlight playing a game of hide and seek behind scudding cloud banks, it offers a unique beauty all its own. Stark and uncompromising, endless waves of heather and tough sedges are constantly buffeted by incessant winds that sweep across this dour landscape.

Remote from even the smallest village, the Tan Hill Inn remains an oasis that has offered comfort and shelter to generations of travellers. Beyond the immediate surroundings of the building, the highest pub in Great Britain at 1732ft (528 metres), only the hardy Swaledale sheep abound; except, of course, for intrepid explorers clutching this G.D. guidebook.

Clear paths can be followed for much of the way, and on a clear day this route is a joy to walk with the added guarantee of a seclusion that should be prized. Everything on this northern rim of the Yorkshire Dales focuses on Tan Hill. In days gone by it was a thriving centre for coal mining and many shafts still remain hidden by the moorland grass so be very careful.

Suffice it to say that the miners made full use of the liquid facilities available at the inn, along with gypsies and cattle drovers who passed this way. Tan Hill is where most of the Dales coal was to be found, the land being under the control of the great monastic houses until their dissolution in the reign of Henry VIII in the 16th century. It was needed primarily to smelt the lead mined in Swaledale and essential for coating their vast roofs.

Tan Hill Inn: highest and loneliest pub in England

Very little evidence remains of the pits that once littered the moors hereabouts although the spirit and essence of those who laboured down the narrow shafts is never far away, drifting like the curlew on rising winds to accompany you on this fine walk.

But it is the inn that attracts most visitors, an unmistakeable landmark visible for miles. Of the numerous licensees to manage the premises, Susan Peacock was the most flamboyant. Not a lady likely to tolerate foolish behaviour on the part of her customers, she is known to have secreted a revolver behind the bar. At least one vandal is known to have been chased off with the sound of gunfire rattling his ears. Although nobody was ever actually shot, as a deterrent it proved to be highly successful.

Ghostly happenings that have plagued the inn down the years are all placed at the feet of Susan Peacock – the pistol-packin' landlady – pictures falling off the wall, the bar till flying open and the beer pumps going down. Nothing serious, so perhaps she approves of how the inn is being run and the popularity it is enjoying.

The current owners employ a generator for electricity and a borehole to provide a regular supply of water. A friend of the landlord who fancied himself as a dowser was spot on about where the hole should be drilled, water being struck at a depth of 170ft. And all done with a twitching stick!

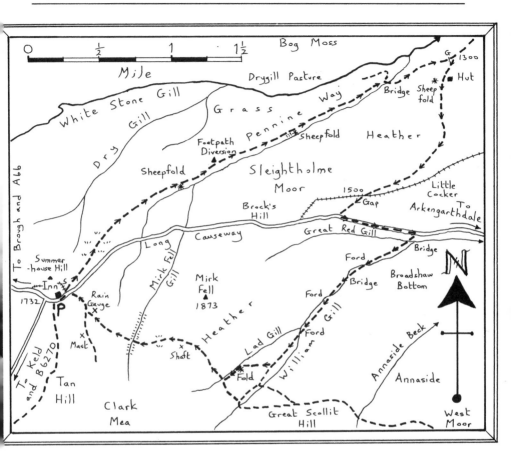

This is definitely not the sort of terrain for a casual country stroll, especially if a thick pea-souper blankets the moors in its damp embrace. Save it for a clear day if only for the distant views, but expect a keen wind even if the weather might be hot and sticky down in the valley bottoms. It is not merely for the benefit of tourists that an open fire is kept burning at the inn throughout the year.

Make full use of the Pennine Way that passes the inn having forged a path over Tan Hill from Swaledale. Cross a fence stile on the right to head off in a north-eastern direction on a thin trail in the grass. After dropping down off Clay Hill, the terrain flattens into a broad plateau that is marshy in places.

Slowly, the depression worn down by the infant Frumming Beck takes shape. Keep to the left side, passing a sheepfold and soon after a large cairn, which marks a diversion from the original right of way. Thereafter, white-topped marker posts clearly indicate the route to be followed. A much drier and easier alternative sticks to this north side of the beck.

The title of Stainmore Forest was clearly given to this flat moorland by a wag sporting a sense of humour, trees being as common as umbrellas in the Sahara. In consequence, the distance covered appears far less than is indeed the case. Keep turning round and the roof of the Tan Hill Inn, left of Summer House Hill, is still there.

Progress will show that the beck cutting is now more pronounced as the convergence with Sleightholme Beck becomes imminent. Eventually a vehicular bridge is reached. Cross the beck and continue on the far side along this major track above the substantial water-worn terracing. Immediately beyond a bar gate, swing sharp right, leaving the Pennine Way to head south along the stony track called Sleightholme Moor Road.

Passing an old green hut and sheepfold on opposite sides, we enter the National Park through a gap in the boundary fence. Another 300 metres will bring you to the fell road. Head left for a half mile until a footpath sign on the right points the way into the hills on the far side.

Another clear track accompanies the ravine of William Gill, switching from side to side over fords and a bridge until the source of the beck is reached at some abandoned mine workings. After 1½ miles, a clear track forks off the valley route to the right and will lead you to Lad Gill. Follow the meandering course of this minor stream on its left bank for 300 metres, until a narrow yet obvious path crosses.

Make a right to follow this route up the gently shelving eastern slope of Mirk Fell. Heading west, the path cuts a clear line through the heather across the broad edge of the fell. Once the opposite flank is reached, take note of the communications station on the near horizon. Your route will pass about 200 metres to the right of this.

Lean to the left past a coal-mining shaft with rusty iron bars over the entrance. The trail then becomes a little indistinct until you approach the deep trough of Mirk Fell Gill, which is crossed without any deviation. Up the far side of the ravine, continue onward along a clear trail that passes a fenced enclosure housing a rain gauge.

Soon after, the thin grass path merges with a major track serving the communications station. Accompany it right down to the fell road where a left will return you to the Tan Hill Inn. And perhaps a celebratory tincture of Theakston's Old Peculiar at this most unique of English pubs – the driver will, of course, restrict his or her consumption to a more suitable beverage.

2. Ravenstonedale

Courting the Peculiar

Mysteries: The Gilbertine Priory, GR 723043; Source of the Lune, GR 701012

Distance Walked: 6½ miles

Total Height Climbed: 1200 feet, 366 metres

Start/Finish: Approaching from Tebay, turn right off the A685 for Ravenstonedale and park at the junction of the first side road on the right.

Terrain: Once the intake fields are left behind, all is open grass moorland across rolling upland fells, with good paths up to Green Bell and beyond Knoutberry.

Nearest Shops: Ravenstonedale

Map Required: Ordnance Survey 1:25000 Howgill Fells sheet

Once described as resembling a quiescent herd of carousing elephants, the Howgill Fells offer a smoothly undulating landscape more in keeping with the Yorkshire Dales than Lakeland. Their gently shelving curvature provides easy walking, and fast progress can be made on tracks that plunge deep into the heart of the fells. Beyond the intake walls, there exist no barriers to free movement.

Only the distant cawing of a lone raven coupled with the amiable chatter from silver-tongued gills are likely to disturb the tranquillity that epitomises this corner of the Howgills, the rolling panorama having changed but little over the centuries. For it is the raven that has given its name to the tiny village nestling in a crook of the northern aspect.

Hauntingly remote and utterly beguiling, the ancient village of Ravenstonedale (pronounced 'razendl') has become even more enticing for the discerning walker since being shunted onto the bachburner by the new bypass. This rapid-transit link route over the Pennine watershed discourages any thought of dalliance by passing motorists.

Perhaps this seclusion encouraged the Gilbertine order of monks to settle here back in the Dark Ages. In those far off days at the start of the last millennium, the order comprising both men and women chose this location to build a priory, the foundations of which can still be seen adjoining the present church of St Oswald's towards the end of this walk.

Make your way up the road that serves Greenside Farm for 100 metres only then head right through a gate and alongside the wall on your left.

Ancient priory foundations adjoining St Oswald's church in Ravenstonedale

Keep with this field track into the next field, after which you will arrive at a walled corridor gated at one end only. Cross the next field until a disintegrating barn is reached. Pass through a gate, changing to the opposite side of the wall. Another gate gives onto a track that drops down to cross Greenside Beck, thereafter keeping right of an old house to gain a metalled farm road.

Now bear left until the accompanying wall veers away to the right. Where the road enters open country, slant left along a tractor track, keeping left around the marshy depression of Tailor Mire. Frequent sightings of fell ponies should inform you that few others of the human race are likely to be encountered hereafter. And should you be unlucky enough to break a leg these noble creatures will be loath to offer assistance, regarding biped interlopers with a tacit disdain.

Indistinct initially, the track heads south-south-west across the grass flank of Pinksey, becoming more pronounced as height is gained. Continue due south up a gradual incline past the lone outpost known as Hunthoof Pike – a clear reference to its equine residents. Just beyond here, leave the

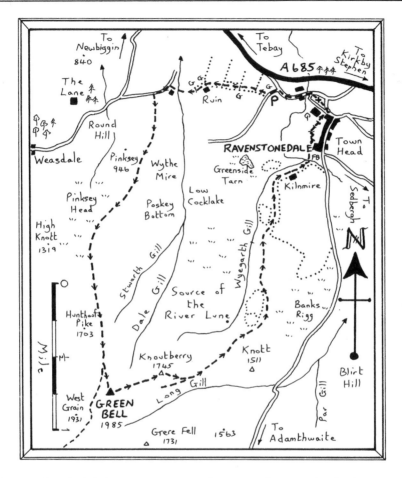

clear trail to fork left to the summit of Green Bell, one of only three in the Howgills that boast a trig column.

The highest peak in the vicinity is Randygill Top, a mile to the south-west, which exceeds the magical 2000ft contour by 47 feet. Green Bell fails to meet this requirement for mountain status by a mere 15 feet. If you cannot resist the temptation to include a 'mountain' in the day's itinerary, a simple path links the two summits and adds two miles to the distance walked.

From Green Bell, head north-east down a gently sloping ridge past a sheepfold on the left. These slopes mark the spring where Dale Gill emerges and the headwaters of the mighty River Lune. One of the north's premiere watercourses, it swings west at Newbiggin, eventually making a dignified exit beyond Lancaster at Sunderland Point, a distance of 70 miles. Streams to the east of Knoutberry, soon reached up a brief rise, feed into Scandal Beck and the River Eden.

From the top of Knoutberry, drop down pathless grass slopes to the south-east, aiming for an obvious path on the far side of the Long Gill valley. Accompany this down under the shadow of Knott, keeping to the right of a walled enclosure. Continue heading due north to reach the first of the intake walls, after which the track strengthens on the approach to the outer 'suburbs' of Ravenstonedale on the right bank of Wyegarth Gill.

Join the second span of a double footbridge ascending a grassy walled lane that opens out in an area of rough grass. Keep with the stony track to a metalled lane, turning left then immediately right along this one for 100 metres. Watch for a stile on the left enabling you to cross to the opposite corner of a small, walled pasture.

Straddle another stile into a vegetable allotment, the right of way being a grass path between the lettuce and cabbage patches. At the far side enter an open field and cross straight over to a gated stile at the opposite side where dense woods are entered. A thin trod cleaves a way through the undergrowth down to a fence stile.

Over this, walk down through the trees to an access lane, following it round to the right then left to gain the main street. Bear left past a second-hand book dealers to fork right past the village school and enter the churchyard through a gate.

At the far side of St Oswald's can be found the excavated remains of the old priory. An unusual sect with their own laws and customs, the Gilbertines are the only true British monastic order, all the others having originated on mainland Europe. Indeed, they came across the Pennines from the East coast in Lincolnshire, where St Gilbert drew a small group around him in 1089. Planning as he went along, the sect arrived in Ravenstonedale and adopted the down-to-earth approach to life that has become synonymous with the county of Yorkshire where many of the brethren originated.

Excavations done in the early part of the 20th century revealed that the monks were particularly fond of shellfish in their diet. Maybe it was their uniquely English approach to religion that influenced the Nonconformist attitude prevalent in later centuries.

The adjacent church is unique in having box pews of oak that face onto the central aisle. One feature that I have never noticed in any other church is an inside clock, doubtless there to ensure the vicar does not overrun his sermonising. One of the stained-glass windows on the east side of the church is in memory of Elizabeth Gaunt, in 1685 the last woman to be burned at the stake for her Nonconformist beliefs.

Noted for benevolent works, the good lady was accused of harbouring traitors by one of those whom she had sheltered. This cowardly action was incited when the blackguard learned that anybody who gave evidence would be pardoned for his crimes. A witness to the sad event claims that when "she had calmly disposed the straw about her in such a manner as to shorten her sufferings, all the bystanders burst into tears".

Another unusual custom that was practised until its final demise in 1623 was the right of sanctuary. Any criminal who entered the portals of the church and managed to toll the bell would not face any charges, no matter how scandalous his transgression. It is little wonder that fugitives from all over the north came to Ravenstonedale to gain an easy remission of their sins. With felons who had committed bloody murder being released back into the community without a stain on their heinous character, it is not surprising that James I decided that something had to be done. And so ended the Right of Sanctuary.

Following on from this association with legal matters is the court held in the church that became known as The Peculiar Court of Ravenstonedale. It was commissioned with the task of implementing the total authority of law within the manor, a duty that was exerted in full measure atop Gallows Hill on the far side of the main road and now known as Park Hill.

The independent spirit of the village residents in the 18th century is colourfully illustrated by a proclamation devised by the young ladies who were annoyed that all the eligible bachelors were looking elsewhere for suitable wives. Their written protest of 1776 stated that any who married other than village girls would be fined £20 and imprisoned. Whether this threat was ever carried out has been lost in the mists of time.

Continue to the far side of the churchyard and out of the gate to cross open grass to another gate at the far side. This brings us out near to the Kings Head, where a left will see you strolling back along the old road to the starting point.

3. Kirkby Stephen

Never a Boaring Moment!

Mystery: The Last Wild Boar, GR 7598

Summits Climbed: Wild Boar Fell 2324 feet, 709 metres; Swarth Fell 2235 feet, 681 metres

Distance Walked: 7 miles

Total Height Climbed: 1550 feet, 473 metres

Start/Finish: Approaching Upper Mallerstang from the direction of Garsdale, park on the roadside pull-in opposite an old quarry located just before the road crosses the railway at Aisgill.

Terrain: Moorland walking in wild surroundings on paths that are often indistinct or non-existent. An exhilarating yomp along the broad ridge.

Nearest Shops: Kirkby Stephen

Map Required: Ordnance Survey 1:25000 Outdoor Leisure 19, Howgill Fells & Upper Eden Valley

Mallerstang is a long tapering valley never more than half a mile wide which commences at the Eden watershed, approximately 200 metres from that of the River Ure, flowing east into Wensleydale. At the head of yet another valley, namely Garsdale, stands the Moor Cock Inn, a remote yet well-known hostelry.

Nowhere is the gradient steep, a feature of the landscape that encouraged engineers to run the prestigious Settle-Carlisle Railway along this route. One of the country's most exciting rural lines, it has survived numerous threats of closure from those who place a well-ordered balance sheet above local needs.

The start of this walk marks the approximate summit of the line, which has climbed a total of 700ft (213 metres) since branching at Settle. Unfortunately, the steam locomotives of my trainspotting youth have long since become museum exhibits, brought out of retirement and dusted down for special occasions only. At such times you are more likely to see photographers lining the most dramatic sections of the route, for that all important shot of an old puffer, than fell wanderers.

Driving up Mallerstang from the south, you cannot fail to be inspired by the grand parade of overhanging gritstone crags along the rim of Wild Boar Fell and its acolytes. The scalloped edge provides a superb high-level tra-

One of the stone men guarding Wild Boar Fell

verse that breaks up the monotony of the surrounding expanse of bleak moorland. And perched on the lip standing guard over the valley are the Stone Men. This platoon of cairns appears to have had the same purpose as the Nine Standards over towards Kirkby Stephen, which is to dissuade invaders from any plunderous intent. From a distance they present the image of watching sentinels, and if they instilled a note of caution into the hearts and minds of advancing hordes, then their construction was not in vain.

Remote from the main tourist trails, the resemblance of Wild Boar to its cousin Ingleborough is apparent throughout – a geological parallel rather than one of popularity as the narrow and often pathless route testifies. Interest is maintained by attempting to identify the changing strata of the underlying rocks from a limestone base through sandstone and shale to the Millstone Grit canopy.

From the old quarry, walk down the road over the Cotegill rail bridge for half a mile to Aisgill Farm. Go through a gate opposite and climb a stony trail to pass under the viaduct spanning Ais Gill, which thunders down a pronounced ravine. Lean right for a short distance then sharp left to follow a grass track that soon fades in the tough moorland grass.

Swing north again to cross a number of gullies along the narrow sheep trod that should eventually bring you to the sloping intake wall above the

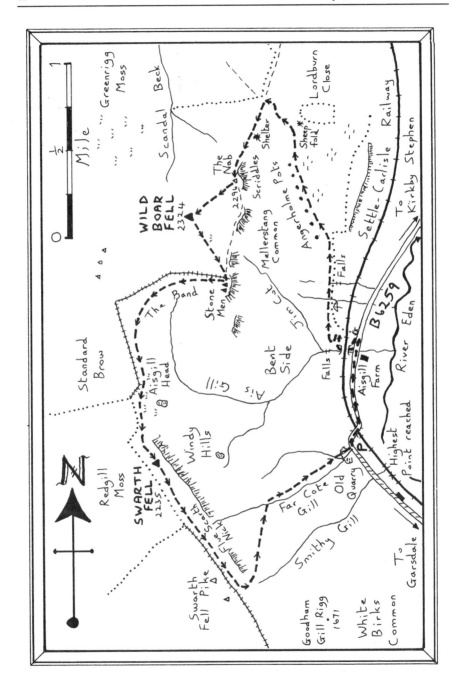

railway. This approach is anything but dull, with avid anticipation of exciting things to come stimulated by the brooding challenge of the Wild Boar skyline known as The Nab.

One of the gullies crossed is noteworthy because of the tree that appears on the other side of the wall. Not a cause for huge celebrations except for the fact that it is the only tree encountered during the entire walk. The second gully is one of those peculiar to limestone country where the watercourse that has disappeared upstream, re-emerges further down, in this case immediately beyond the wall.

When the wall veers to the right, lean slightly left to join a line of crater holes known as Angerholme Pots. Close inspection of these fluted sinks to the west of the limestone plateau will provide ample opportunity for you to decide whether potholing is an activity worthy of more investigation at some later date. Miners and sewer inspectors will doubtless pass on quickly. After all, it is their day off!

Those who choose to linger should, however, beware. Nowhere else in the vicinity is there such a variety of access points to the subterranean world. Open to public view, the ever-present danger of a careless slip could result in confinement within these lonely dungeons. Holes in the ground are best left to the likes of Bugs Bunny so steer a course along the right-hand edge of the pots, across the disintegrating limestone pavement.

Close-cropped turf makes the walking easy even though the path is indistinct. Make for a clear groove that angles across the steeply shelving flank ahead. En route, stay 100 metres to the left of a ruined sheepfold adjoining a walled enclosure. Keep your eye on the 'notched' profile of The Nab and try to determine what mythical creature it conjures up in your mind.

Once the wall on the ridge is reached, bear left following a clear path along the rim up to the gnarled outcropping of The Nab, there to stand atop the wild boar's head and survey the ancestral domain where his final stand was made. Like the summit plateau of High Street in Lakeland, shepherds used to indulge in horseracing across the broad span.

The name itself stems from the ferocious beast that struck fear into the guts of simple Dales folk in Medieval England. Its tusks were prized as a symbolic triumph of light over the forces of darkness. Legend suggests that as the boar population fell into decline, the last in line sought shelter on these bleak and windswept fells of the Upper Eden.

A poet of the day claimed that a certain Philip Hartley chased the boar onto the plateau above Aisgill, whereupon the cornered beast turned to protect itself. Both the hunter and his dogs were slain, after which a giant pursued the boar to the very summit:

'The giant with one stroke on loins
Deprived the boar of life,
Which gave a title to the hill
That ne'er will pass away,
For it is called Wild Boar Fell
E'en to this very day.'

All very lyrical and measured, but the most likely scenario is that Richard de Musgrave who died in 1409 delivered the fatal blow. And this is when the name of Wild Boar Fell was first adopted. Added credence was given to this supposition in 1847 when the great man's tomb was being restored in Kirkby Stephen Church. Inside were two large boar tusks beside the skeleton. This slaying of the last boar in England is said to mark the turning point when the Dark Ages of fear and superstition surrendered to a more enlightened epoch.

From The Nab, slant half right across the flat tableland to reach the actual summit of the fell. Few people bother to make this diversion, erroneously assuming that the Stone Men mark the summit. I once found myself wandering aimlessly across this featureless expanse in thick mist and snow and never did locate the highest point. That was in my impetuous youth when such challenges were the norm and eagerly embraced. Middle age has fostered a more circumspect approach to impulsive actions on the fells. And you are advised to do likewise.

From the trig column ensconced within a small shelter, head south-east towards the gritstone phalanx. Cross a fence stile to join this piece of bellicose chicanery overlooking the rock-strewn battleground in the amphitheatre below. From here follow a thin path that circles around the head of Ais Gill known as The Band, dropping gradually down into the depression at Aisgill Head.

Join the wall, keeping right of a tarn to cross the marshy hollow. Stick with the wall that climbs up onto Swarth Fell, the summit cairn being located left of the main path. Beyond here, continue straight ahead across a shallow depression onto Swarth Fell Pike at the end of the ridge. Here the wall and then a fence mark the edge of the Yorkshire Dales boundary.

Immediately after the second cairn on the far side of the fence, make a wide left-hand swing down an easy grass bank and over Aisgill Moor. A north-easterly bearing will bring you to the cutting of Far Cote Gill, easily identified by tracing its course down from Flue Scarth Nick.

Cross to the far side and pick up a thin trod that follows the gill down, culminating in a waterfall debouching into the old quarry. Take care on this final descent to the road, the bare rock wall being steep and treacherous in wet weather. There is no excuse for unnecessary injuries sustained at the culmination of such a fine walk.

4. Muker

Bring Out Your Dead!

Mystery: The Old Corpse Road
Distance Walked: 6 miles
Total Height Climbed: 650 feet, 198 metres
Start/Finish: Make use of the official car park adjacent to the bridge over Straw Beck at the eastern end of Muker.
Terrain: A clear miners' track links Muker with Keld along the valley of Upper Swaledale, with a delightful high-level return along the old corpse road. Rough walking but nowhere too steep.
Nearest Shops: Muker
Map Required: Ordnance Survey 1:25000 Outdoor Leisure 30, Northern & Central areas

Perhaps on account of its remoteness, or even the compressed nature of the elongated glacial trough, Swaledale has always been less accessible than the other major dales. It has been likened to a separate little country in its own right and the River Swale squeezes between steeply shelving grass flanks ranged with limestone scarring. Together with the extensive tracts of rough moorland, this wild terrain conspires to hinder the casual traveller in his quest for the elusive valley of the Swale.

Those daring individuals who persevere will be rewarded with a dale of intimate charm and fascination unlike any other. Small villages cluster along the valley bottoms at regular intervals. Muker is the most popular in Upper Swaledale and it is easy to understand why after a brief stroll around its nooks and corners. Stone cottages are scattered randomly above the road to avoid the possibility of flooding as a result of the village's proximity to the confluence of Straw Beck with the Swale.

June is the month to visit this part of Swaledale, when the proliferation of buttercups creates an ocean of yellow that is breathtaking to behold. Here at Muker the valley swings abruptly north, assuming a distinctively alpine character that has been referred to as the 'English Tyrol'. The isolated 'island hill' of Kisdon, which is almost completely surrounded by watercourses, effectively divides Swaledale in two, the road continuing ahead through Thwaite and onward to the head of the valley at Keld.

Our walk up this hidden section of the dale to the east of Kisdon makes for a splendid link route with Keld, the secluded hamlet where the old

The old corpse road passed through Muker

corpse road had its origins. The whole journey through Muker and the other villages terminated at Grinton, which was the only church in Swaledale with a consecrated graveyard (see walk 6). Corpses were carried in wicker baskets to save weight on the arduous two-day journey.

Turning up the lane from the main road, our way passes by the church whose own consecrated ground had been long awaited by the local citizens. Built in 1580, it was only one of a handful that appeared during the first Elizabethan era and brought to an end the protracted journey along the corpse road. Follow the signposts, leaning right to enter the fields behind the huddle of cottages.

A narrow, flagged footway leads through the lower pastures, negotiating a number of gated stiles to arrive at the limit of the enclosed in-bye land. Each has its own byre for cattle to winter in and there are sixty within half a mile of Muker. On either side, wooded slopes soar skyward, supporting the alpine association.

Once the last stile has been crossed you will have reached the riverbank, so bear right over another stile and so onto the footbridge spanning the Swale. At the far side, fork left up the steep banking to join the main track from Gunnerside. Now head north along this old miners' road, following the course of the river upstream.

Even the most 'optically challenged' of walkers will experience great difficulty getting lost on this route, which will eventually, after 1½ miles, bring you to the awesome cleft of Swinner Gill. This mighty split gives the impression that the giant hand of some primeval Goliath has attempted to hack a mammoth chunk out of the valley side at this point. The result is a rent of devastating proportions, at the head of which are the old lead mines visited on Walk 5.

The path swings into the lower recesses of the gorge where a footbridge enables the gill to be crossed dry-footed. Thereafter, it climbs up towards the wooded slopes cloaking Bracken Hill, entered through a gate. The acclivitous valley sides have recently been planted with new saplings to prevent erosion of the soil. Our route, now heading north-west, continues onward to Keld at this higher level, thus avoiding the constricted flow of the river in the pinched valley below.

Once the woods are left behind the gradient eases, with Crackpot Hall hidden from view on the slopes above. No hideout for the lunatic fringe as the name might imply, this locale was less remote in days gone by than now, due to the constant passage of miners heading for Swinner Gill. Today the National Trust is renovating the old farmstead; an essential undertaking if the structure is to remain upright as the oblique nature of the land has caused the walls to tilt at ungainly angles.

Little now remains of the forest that once swathed the valley sides and where the Lord of the Manor hunted prodigious herds of red deer. Only after 1725 did these sensitive creatures finally abandon the valley, when their arboreal habitat died off from the fumes emitted by the lead-smelting mills. The presence of this valuable mineral also meant that hens could not survive at Crackpot Hall on account of lead poisoning. The inevitable price of progress.

Soon after passing the access track serving the hall, our path kinks to the left across a broad gully below the abandoned workings of Beldi Hill Lead Mines. It then descends gradually to a gate above Kisdon Force, a fine waterfall only accessible from valley level. Soon after, the accompanying fence on the left veers away downhill as the track continues on to reach a wide footbridge spanning East Gill. This is another ravine that scores a furrow deep into the heart of Hall Moor, the summit of which is Rogan's Seat at 2204ft (672 metres).

Just beyond the tree-girt beck, watch for the sharp left turn down to the footbridge over the Swale. The valley is deeply enclosed at this point; the climb out being up a loose gravelly path before easing for the walk into Keld along a rough-walled lane. It emerges on the main square of what is little more than a large hamlet. Highest of the Swaledale settlements, its location away from the main road was no accidental occurrence. Viking settlers

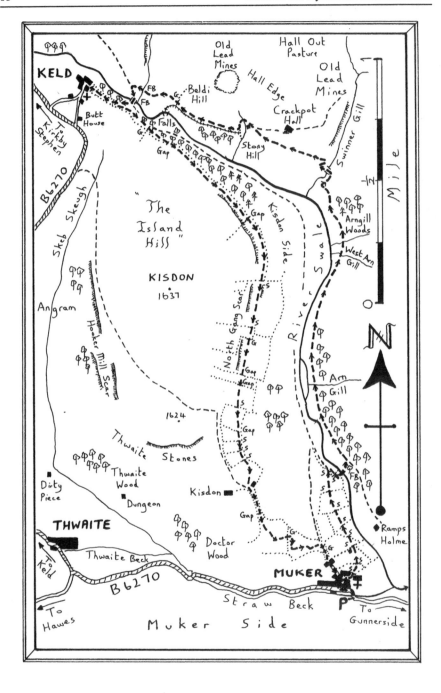

chose the hollow for safety from rampaging hordes of Celtic brigands sweeping down from the north. Unseen from the normal line of march, Keld was left in peace – as, indeed, is the case today when motorists pass it by unknowingly.

Most interesting of the buildings for our purpose is the Congregational Chapel that sports a fine sun clock on the wall above the door. And it certainly is accurate as you will discover should you have the good fortune to arrive when our guiding star has elected to make one of his rare appearances. The chapel has been rebuilt on numerous occasions. Edward Stillman is the best-remembered cleric to officiate here.

He was resident incumbent for a total of 48 years from 1789, after wandering about Swaledale trying to find a permanent home. An epic journey that he made to London raised the princely sum of £700 to renovate the crumbling chapel, and being a frugal parson he did it at a cost to himself of only sixpence (2.5 pence). None of the village's deceased were buried here officially although the poorest citizens who could not afford the cost of a proper funeral were interred in nearby fields. Those lucky enough to have the wherewithal were manhandled all the way down the valley to the only consecrated ground at Grinton.

Another character of note is 'Neddy Dick' who devised a musical instrument made from stones of varying weights and sizes selected from the bed of the Swale. According to reports handed down, the tunes played on this home-made dulcimer could actually be recognised by the audience.

Returning down the walled track that marks the start of the corpse road, keep to the higher level and ignore all paths forking left down into the valley bottom. After passing through a gate, the original course of the corpse road leans right through another gate, keeping above the wall that fringes the wooded slopes. Now fallen into disuse, purists can still follow it until the main path joins in higher up by means of gap in the wall.

This route around the upper reaches of Kisdon avoided the dense woodland in the valley, which was on the boggy side and far more extensively forested than today. Although more exposed to the elements, the portage of dead bodies was easier on the open ground. Large flat rocks were placed at regular intervals to rest the wicker baskets.

In addition to those actually carrying the 'dear departed', mourners and the family trudged behind, making a long procession. Rest and recuperation was made available at various taverns, where toasting the life of the deceased was carried on long into the night. On one occasion, such was the inebriated condition of the coffin-bearers that they picked up the wrong cadaver and only discovered their mistake when the lids were raised. Calvert Houses and Shoregill Head towards Ivelet were hostelries that have since reverted to their original farming traditions.

Wooden coffins were only introduced after 1716 when the Vicar of Muker refused to bury any more of his flock in wicker baskets. Even when the church at Muker became consecrated, the corpse road was still used to carry the bodies from outlying farms, the superstition persisting for many years after that the dead would not rest if they were taken along any other road.

Accompany the corpse road along the level trail south and over a number of stiles until it begins to descend the south-east shoulder above Muker. Aim to the right of a lone barn at the bottom of the field to enter a walled corridor. After passing through a gap in the wall 200 metres down, the obvious half-paved track meanders downhill in a series of loops. At the bottom, bear right through a gate into a lane at the edge of Muker.

The corpse road continues beyond Muker, heading east up the valley and fording the river close to its junction with Straw Beck. It then negotiates the lower slopes of Ivelet Side and goes through Gunnerside towards its final destination at Grinton Church.

Our terminus is the Farmers Arms on Muker's main street, where a toast to the completion of a blue-ribbon exploration of Upper Swaledale can be savoured at leisure.

5. Gunnerside Gill
Lead Me to the Mines

Mysteries: Gunnerside Gill, Swinner Gill Kirk, GR 912014

Distance Walked: 8 miles with Swinner Gill Kirk

Total Height Climbed: 950 feet, 290 metres with Swinner Gill Kirk

Start/Finish: Parking is available on the open fell road above the hamlet of Ivelet, close to Dykes Head.

Terrain: Rough moorland terrain with clear paths all the way. No steep climbing unless you elect to visit Swinner Gill Kirk.

Nearest Shops: Muker

Map Required: Ordnance Survey 1:25000 Outdoor Leisure 30, Yorkshire Dales, Northern & Central areas

Forging deep into the northern flank of Swaledale, the trench of Gunnerside Gill has long been associated with lead mining on a grand scale. The days when the area was a thriving industrial community have long since departed. Today the decaying remnants of a dead industry harbour only the memory and spirit of miners who grafted long and hard in the subterranean galleries.

In days long since confined to the history books, miners had to walk many miles to their work and often stopped for a smoke of twist tobacco, knitting scarves to pass the time. "Let's sit down for six needles," became an oft-quoted expression from those in need of a rest. But the industry took a heavy toll in lives when 'health and safety at work' was unheard of. Many departed this mortal coil before their appointed time, local graveyards being the final resting place for young men cut off in their prime by the scourge of lead poisoning.

Above the mine workings, the vast tract of heather-clad moorland is home to the much-maligned red grouse. Butts and shooting boxes testify to the popularity of this fine game bird in the sights of the hunting fraternity. So if it is peace and tranquillity that attracts you to the heights above Gunnerside, avoid this walk on the 'glorious twelfth' (of August). This controversial day heralds the start of the shooting season, when decibel output increases radically from shotgun volleys pouring skywards.

Our walk begins up the old mine road slanting north-east across the open fell. It then swings north into the enclosed confines of Gunnerside Gill. The clear track maintains a level course under the lyrically titled Jingle Pot Edge

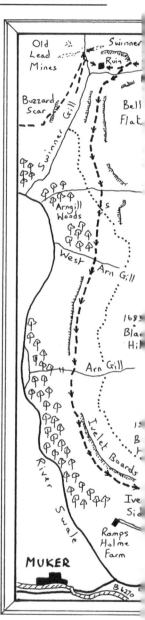

before curving left into the side valley of Botcher Gill. Beyond a wall gate the gill is crossed by a substantial bridge, thereafter continuing up the fell over Lowanthwaite towards the mass of spoil waste from the lead excavations.

Generations of lead miners, often from the same family, toiled underground by candlelight in appalling conditions. Sometimes the evidence pointing to a likely seam would come to nought, the caustic response being, "T'Auld Man's bin 'ere afore us!" This meant that other miners had worked there previously and dug out all the worthwhile ore.

Any strange occurrences or ghostly appearances were always laid on the shoulders of *T'Auld Man*, a name given to all the miners who had struggled over the years to wrest a living from this highly volatile terrain. Superstition was rife and witch stones (akin to polo mints threaded with string) have been found in the workings. They were hung throughout the cramped passageways to ward off any malignant influence that might infect the mines and bring bad luck to those who worked there.

Like many of the old traditional industries, the mines were forced to shut down around 1880 when cheaper imports of lead began to arrive from Spain. Following the industry's demise, many of the families dependent on the lead mining decamped from Swaledale altogether and moved to Lancashire. But it was not long before a similar fate was to befall that county's textile industry. For a full history of the dale's lead mining industry, a visit to the museum at Reeth will be time well spent prior to setting out on this walk.

When the track swings away to the north alongside a fence up to Rogan's Seat, keep ahead along a grass concourse over a fence stile. A fenced tarn is passed on the right as the track heads west down the right side of East Grain. It steepens appreciably entering the rugged confines of Swinner Gill. Our route crosses the tumbling beck to follow a thin trail on the far side, opposite a cluster of ruined mine buildings.

T'Auld Man has clearly had a field day around here. Those with an excess of energy and the spirit of adventure may wish to visit Swinner Gill Kirk by passing the mine buildings and veering right up the ravine of Hind

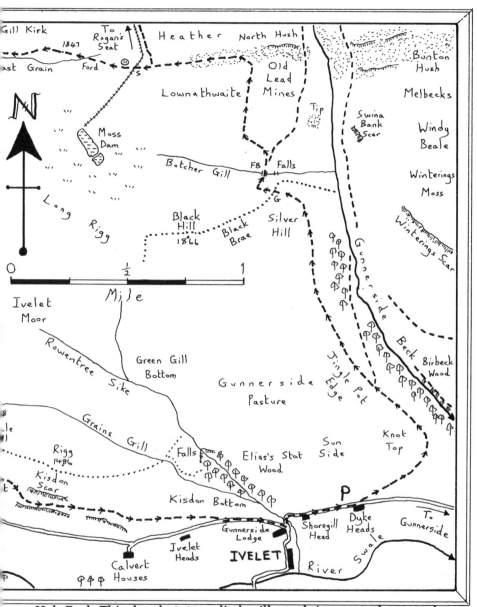

Hole Beck. This short but steep climb will soon bring you to the cave where Puritan clergy ministered to their Nonconformist flock before freedom of worship was granted in 1689.

T'Auld Man has much to answer for in the lead mines above Swinner Gill

Religious texts once adorned the walls of the cave, but time and the elements have long since erased these. Lookouts would keep a wary eye on the fellside above to give warning of approaching danger in the form of government inquisitors sent to root out any seditious gatherings. This detour from the main route should be attempted only in dry conditions and not when the beck is in spate.

The path bends south along a terrace into the upper valley of the River Swale. Beyond a wall stile, the next two miles follow a truly delightful course along the steep flanks of the valley between low crags of limestone scarring. Every step is a joy to walk so take the time to fully appreciate the firm underlying foundations as the path meanders through remarkable scenery of the highest quality. On the opposite side of the deeply enclosed valley of the Upper Swale is the old corpse route which we will be following on Walk 4.

Beyond a deviation into the stony gully of West Arn Gill, the way passes through an extended conurbation of rabbit warrens that conjure up images of Watership Down countryside. Once Kisdon Scar is left behind, the indistinct path gradually loses height heading east above Muker to eventually merge with the metalled access road serving Ramps Holme Farm. Stick with this past Gunnerside Lodge, bending sharp left down over Grain Gill before climbing back up the open road for a further quarter mile back to Dykes Head.

6. Grinton

Murder Most Horrid

Mystery: The Scottish Laird, GR 047984

Distance Walked: 6½ miles

Total Height Climbed: 900 feet, 274 metres

Start/Finish: The main street in Grinton is sufficiently wide adjacent to the church to allow cars to park.

Terrain: Bleak, heather-clad moors are pockmarked with the detritus of the once prolific lead mining industry. Clear tracks make for easy route selection.

Nearest Shops: Reeth

Map Required: Ordnance Survey 1:25000 Outdour Leisure 30, Northern & Southern areas

Few villages can claim a greater association with the afterlife than Grinton. Over shadowed by the larger neighbouring settlement of Reeth, which houses a fine museum dedicated to the folk heritage of Swaledale, Grinton enjoys a somewhat macabre past where coffins, corpses and cadavers play key roles. The churchyard was the terminus of a celebrated corpse road that began at Keld higher up the valley (See Walk 4) and only fell into disuse after the church at Muker was consecrated.

Grinton Church is also unusual in having a number of tiny windows at its eastern end. These were known as 'lepers' squint' apertures and enabled afflicted members of the congregation to take part in the service without affecting those inside. These minute, leaded openings afford an unrestricted view of the altar where mass was performed. Another opinion as to their purpose is that outside observers could give warning to late-comers that the service was about to begin. But whatever the origins of these singular orifices, there is no denying the beauty and aristocratic bearing that has earned for this church the title 'Cathedral of the Dales'.

People travelled long distances to attend mass at Grinton Church, a factor that contributed to the holding of bi-annual fairs on the Sabbath – commerce and communion occurring in tandem. Yet even before the village became the focus of life in Swaledale, the Romans recognised its importance by establishing a fort close by, commandeering local labour to mine the rich veins of lead.

Grinton is situated at a key point in the dale where the softer aspect of

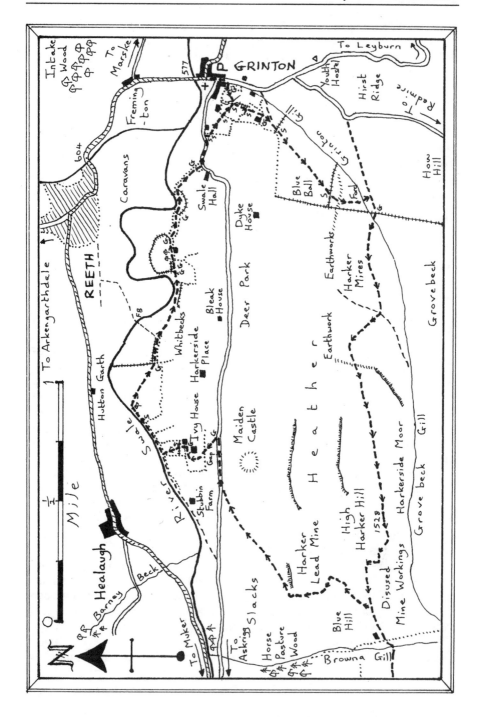

undulating cultivated land surrenders to the harsher wilderness of the upper dale as defined in the Domesday Book of Norman times. Today the landscape is less severe, having absorbed man's influence over the centuries. The ravages of the dominant mining phase that affected much of the Swaledale topography have largely blended into the moorland from which the lead was wrested. These scattered reminders are brought vividly to life at the museum in Reeth, which is well worth a visit.

One mystery that was never satisfactorily resolved concerns the avarice displayed by those who placed money above human life – the result being a foul murder over the moor near Askrigg. Following the sales of cattle at one of the fairs, a certain Scottish Laird was aiming to cross the moor into Swaledale on his way back to Scotland. A pair of conniving local yokels, eaten up with jealousy and greed, waylaid the hapless traveller just beyond Askrigg at Newbiggin. There they did for him in a most diabolical fashion, hiding the bloodstained corpse in a barn prior to burying it on the moor. Unfortunately for them, a courting couple who threatened to 'blow the gaff' witnessed the heinous crime. A share in the loot soon changed their minds, although the hush money proved to be little consolation when all their sheep were drowned in a flood.

Suspicion hung over the rascally pair of felons but no firm evidence could be brought to gain a conviction. Many years after, the Scotsman's body was identified by its tartan covering, which the peat had preserved. One story tells of a spectral Scotsman appearing to a woman in the bedroom of the house where the cadaver was once secreted.

Could this have been a certain Ralph Harker found buried in the peat moss on Whitaside in 1797 as some agencies have suggested? A doubtful suppostion, Harker being a name peculiar to this part of Swaledale and decidedly un-Scottish. The remains of this mysterious person were eventually buried in Grinton cemetery.

Walk up the road from Grinton Church and 50 metres beyond the T-junction, bear right up a short track with a gate at the top end. Make a half-left over the field down to an ancient slabbed footbridge and go through the wall stile. Then it's hard left alongside the fence up to a stile as we begin the ascent of the valley side.

Continue ahead, aiming to the left of a prominent barn and go through the gate nearby. Forking into a clear track ascending from the left, accompany this until a fence stile is reached. Power onward and up the open heather-clad slope as the intake wall veers away to the right. Stick to this trail heading south-west until another fence is reached, one of many that enclose these lower slopes.

Immediately beyond the fence stile, the clear track bisects the remnant of a primeval 'earthwork' dating from the dawn of man's colonisation of this wild terrain. Drop down the far side into a depression to ford Grovebeck Gill and go up the far side to join a major fell track. Lean right through a gate, recrossing the beck and leaving behind the obstructive presence of the fencing to stride out over the bleak wilderness of Harkerside Moor.

The track, once used by miners to reach the lead workings, now offers a fine upland route for walkers . Following an east-west bearing it circumnavigates Gibbon Hill, connecting all the mines on this side of the valley. At the first junction of paths, head north-west to mount Low Harker Hill in front. Bending to the left the track breaks through another 'earthwork' to gain the level plateau of High Harker Hill.

To the south, the bleak featureless expanse of heather moor rises gradually to its apex atop Gibbon Hill. Not the sort of terrain in which to break a leg or you could become a permanent resident in the manner of the ill-fated Ralph Harker, your bones pecked clean by foraging flyers and bleached white by the driven snow.

So keep to the track as it descends the north facing slope of Harker Hill between the amalgam of disused mine workings. About 150 metres short of the cross-fell wall and an isolated stone building, make a sharp right along a branch track that swings clearly down, eventually merging with the fell road above Stubbin Farm. Above us and unseen from this position, the foundations of Maiden Castle with the outlying earth bankings testify to this being a defensive site in prehistoric times.

Stroll along the road heading east towards Grinton for 300 metres until the access track serving Ivy House is reached. Wheel hard left through a gate and down the track, passing through a wall gap, then go left of the house. The track swings right below through another gap and along to a secluded house teetering on this steep flank overlooking the River Swale.

Drop down to a gate abutting the house then aim half left to mount a fence stile and so down to the far left corner of the field, where the riverside trail is joined. Heading downstream, the narrow path has collapsed in places due to undercutting of the bank. After mounting a stile the path enters an open field hugging the riverbank for a further 200 metres. At a tiny clutch of trees lean half right across to the far corner, passing through a gate into a broad corridor.

With a fence and parallel beck to the left, stroll alongside the wall on the right before entering more open grassland. Keep left of the hummocky terrain to reach a loop of the Swale. With a fence now on the right, accompany the river until it swings away once again. Beyond a gate, follow the fence on the left to a corner that conceals another gate.

At its far side, a wall/tree-lined passage is taken past a barn prior to dropping down to a more enclosed corridor. Go through the gate and keep with

Near the end of the old corpse road at Grinton

this section of track all the way to its emergence on the road. Take a left towards Grinton for 200 metres then watch for a stile on the right just beyond a kink in the road.

A short link beside the wall will bring you to another stile giving entry to the adjacent field. Crossing the next two fields, which are both stiled, will bring you to the point where the outward route is to be retraced after crossing the minute slabbed footbridge.

Return to the 'Cathedral of the Dales' and the opportunity to reflect on desolate scenery that characterises much of the landscape above the valley in-take fields. It is little wonder that numerous travellers came to grief when attempting to cross the moors on foot with no assistance from the Ordnance Survey or highway authorities. Ensure that you are not one of them!!

7. Garsdale

One Helluva Jump

Mysteries: Turpin's Leap, GR 786969; Lunds Church, GR 794946
Distance Walked: 6 miles
Total Height Climbed: 550 feet, 168 metres
Start/Finish: Aisgill Moor Cottages are located exactly on the border between Cumbria and North Yorkshire. Driving north from Garsdale Head and the Moor Cock Inn, turn right here along a rough track serving the farm of Hell Gill. Park on the left just before the railway bridge.
Terrain: Rough grassland on the valley sides scarred by deep ravines carved from the limestone bedrock. The only difficult section is that through the reeds below Lunds where the paths are scanty.
Nearest Shops: Garsdale
Map Required: Ordnance Survey 1:25000 Outdoor Leisure 19, Howgill Fells & Upper Eden Valley

It may come as a surprise to many visitors to learn that the Dales' premiere valley of Wensleydale has its origin high up on Mallerstang Fell. For it is these bleak eastern slopes overlooking Garsdale Head that the infant Ure girds up for its epic journey to the North Sea. And no more than 100 metres away lies the source of the River Eden which meanders north to swell the girth of the Irish Sea. So within this remote outpost of lime-washed hills and tough moorland sedges a significant watershed is crossed within the space of a few minutes.

The main road paralleling the renowned Settle-Carlisle Railway has taken over from twin bridleways on either side of the dale head that were once the major thoroughfares. Abandoned farmsteads testify to the bleak nature of the terrain where life was a constant battle for the agricultural communities that lived here. Today only memories within the bare shells remain as a testament to the passage of travellers who negotiated this lonely upland fastness.

Stroll up the track beside Aisgill Moor Cottages to cross the railway bridge. This point marks the border between two counties, the limit of the Yorkshire Dales National Park and the highest elevation of this prestigious railway. Accompany the track round, forking right when the bridleway continues ahead over Hellgill Beck.

We make the crossing of the beck higher up by a bridge, this track being the access to Hell Gill Farm. Go through the gate adjacent to the farm and up the continuing track to reach Lady Ann's Highway. This well-graded route was named after Lady Ann Clifford who controlled much of the land in the valley and made substantial renovations to Pendragon Castle further down Mallerstang.

Two gates and a right wheel will find you peering over the parapet of Hell Gill Bridge into the gloomy depths of the awesome ravine. Shrouded by overhanging trees, it is difficult to ascertain the true nature of this fearsome cleft hewn from the valley side. Certainly it was a major obstacle in times past and prevented vehicular traffic from using the route until the construction of the sturdy edifice that now spans the gulf.

Most famous of the horsemen to jump across Hell Gill was the notorious highwayman Dick Turpin whilst being pursued after a heinous robbery near Hawes. Legend suggests that he and an accomplice fled the scene of the crime with their booty, hoping to evade capture once they crossed the border into Westmorland. Their route took them north from Garsdale Head to Shaw Paddock, which was then a public house. Here they left the valley road, taking to the moors to confuse the pursuers. On reaching the ravine of Hell Gill, the wooden bridge had rotted away. Keeping his horse calm, Turpin spurred him forward for the mighty leap, clearing the fearful chasm by a full metre.

Crossing the deep ravine of Hell Gill

But his partner was not so lucky. The lathered steed panicked at the last moment and plunged with its rider down into the churning maelstrom below, from where they were instantly swept away. The body was discovered a mile downstream some days later. Dick Turpin escaped to continue his nefarious activities elsewhere, but the stolen gold carried by Black Carew was never recovered.

Perhaps it is still there secreted in a remote crevice, just waiting for some intrepid adventurer to descend the brooding fissure. Will you be the lucky one to find Dick Turpin's loot?

If not then push on, heading south-south-east along a broad, grassy concourse and forking left after 100 metres to take the less noticeable bifurcation along 'The Highway'. Keep above the intake walls, fording a number of distinct limestone cuttings en route. After a mile, and one such ford, the first abandoned farmstead of High Hall is passed. Now a broken frame, its naked torso exposed to the rampant elements, this once proud dwelling will have offered food and shelter to travellers when the road was in full use.

A further quarter mile along The Highway a small limekiln is passed on the left, followed soon after by a gate 200 metres beyond. The path then bends left into the widest of the ravines, climbing out to pass through a fence gate and so on to the next abandoned farm of High Dyke. And it is here that we leave Lady Ann's Highway, passing through a gate on the right and another at the rear of the farmyard.

Descend the steepening grass bank through a trio of small, walled fields, emerging into a large open tract dominated by waist-high reeds. A path cuts through these, veering left towards Blades in the valley bottom. As the lower wall is reached, swing right along this to follow it across the reed bed for a quarter mile.

Just beyond a minor stream, mount a wall stile slanting half right up the facing slope to straddle another after 100 metres. Cresting Cowshaw Hill, keep right of the indeterminate summit, ploughing a course through the dense tract of reeds that cloak the knoll. This is unusual in that reeds are normally associated with marshy terrain where drainage is poor, and not, as in this case, with a hill.

Drop down the far side to enter the lonely graveyard of Lunds Church by a stile. Long since abandoned to the sheep that graze between the teetering tombstones, the small church could easily be mistaken for a barn. Established as a chapel-of-ease in 1600, it fell into disuse earlier in the 20th century as more and more farms were abandoned and the resident population declined.

One of the most colourful characters of recent times to attend Lunds Church was Scott Macfie who arrived after the First World War to live at

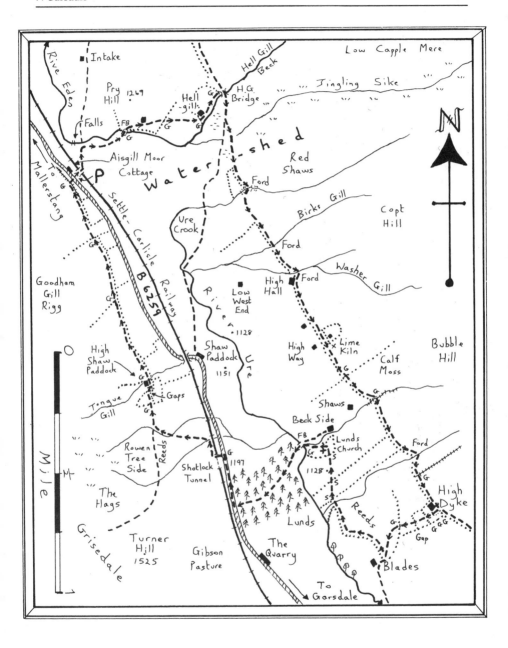

Shaws, higher up the fellside. He was a practical man with all manner of strange ideas and tried to induce a more acceptable form of religion by suggesting that the vicar play football with locals after morning service. Could this have been where the Sunday League began?

To the simple Dales folk Macfie was an eccentric, especially when he invited gypsies to stay on his land. Some claim that his ghost roams the fellside in the vicinity of Lunds although it is more likely to be that of 'Thread Jack', a pedlar who met his end in mysterious circumstances that have never been explained.

Both men were buried in the churchyard, Macfie passing over in 1935. It says something for the influence he manifested when the coffin was draped in a Union Jack and accompanied by a substantial number of mourners. How they all managed to squeeze inside the tiny building for the funeral remains a mystery in its own right.

At the far side of the church, bear left alongside the wall down to a gate. Then cross the footbridge spanning the burgeoning girth of the newly born River Ure and walk up the track through Lunds Plantation to the valley road. Lean right towards Aisgill for 300 metres, taking the gated track on the left over the railway at this end of Shotlock Tunnel.

Continue north alongside the railway for 50 metres until a shallow depression is crossed. Then fork half left up the rising incline, forging through another crop of reeds. Keep to the right side of a narrow stream cutting until the bridleway from Grisedale is joined. Head towards the jutting beak of Wild Boar Fell that dominates the northern prospect on this side of the valley. It is a marvellously enigmatic profile, the challenge of which should be taken up on Walk 3.

After passing through a wall gate, aim to the right side of yet another abandoned farmstead – this one going by the name of High Shaw Paddock. The loneliness of this austere location might explain why one particular farmer and his wife moved to Appersett near Hawes. There they chose to be buried behind the house, not wishing to be interred in consecrated ground. A tombstone marks the site of this bizarre request.

A pair of wall gaps followed by a gate will find you nudging the crumbling ruins, after which the path keeps above the intake wall for the last mile back to Aisgill Moor Cottages. The last gate leads down to the road and straight over up the Hell Gill access track back to the car.

8. Dentdale
A Terrible Place to Visit

Mysteries: The Terrible Knitters, GR 7086; The Sedgewick Stone, GR 705870; The Vampire's Grave, GR 706871

Distance Walked: 5 miles

Total Height Climbed: 900 feet, 274 metres

Start/Finish: An official pay & display car park is available at the western end of Dent.

Terrain: Clear paths all the way along the old and new trails in Dentdale, combining fell and valley scenery.

Nearest Facilities: Dent

Map Required: Ordnance Survey 1:25000 Outdoor Leisure 2, Yorkshire Dales Western Area

Reluctant to advertise its multifarious attributes to the world, Dentdale maintains a low profile that only serves to enhance its allure to the discerning traveller. No extrovert pretensions here. Indeed, Dent Town tries its level best to make life difficult for that most coveted of 20th century icons – the car. Cobbled streets that twist and turn help keep the settlement firmly within its true era, clearly a throwback to a bygone age of simplicity.

Perhaps the appendage of 'town' is a somewhat optimistic euphemism in the new millennium, although it certainly was the principal focus of valley life in the 19th century, being double the size of Sedbergh. Finding itself tucked away in this remote situation ensured that growth was minimal, the village existing in a time warp having withdrawn from the outside world.

Picturesque and quaint, enchanting and unique – lyrical descriptions that continue to attract visitors to Dent's fairytale setting. One event, however, that was definitely not an invention of the little people and which is re-enacted every year relates to the industry that set Dent apart from its contemporaries.

Production of all manner of knitted goods was a universal occupation in the village during the 18th century. And such was the quality of the finished products that locals became known as The Terrible Knitters of Dent. An opposite meaning frequently adopted by today's youth when referring to something exceptionally good, the knitting needles clicked away from dawn 'til dusk, and beyond.

Everybody was a knitter, even the children were taught the skills along-

"Terrible" things happened in Dent

side the 3Rs in school. To help maintain a fast rate of production, folk ballads were sung, often about the Swaledale sheep that supplied the wool. Gloves were the most sought after item, with buyers' names being sewn into the pattern. Today only the memories remain kept alive by a small band of enthusiasts who assiduously extol the accomplishments of their forebears.

Sedgwick is a common name in Dent, the most famous owner being a certain Adam who boasts a splendid memorial to his achievements down the cobbled road from the Sun Hotel. On a corner adjacent to the church access path stands a huge block of granite incorporating a fountain with the great man's name carved thereon. From this site he is known to have enthusiastically proclaimed Nelson's victory over the French navy at Trafalgar back in 1815. In the old days the upper floors of the cottages had 'galleries' built which were used as workrooms by the knitters. Sedgwick commented on this phenomenon, saying that they "almost shut out the light of the sky from those who travelled on the pavement", forming "a highway of communication to a dense and industrious population".

Inside the church of St Andrew, a wall plaque informs us that Adam was a Professor of Geology at Cambridge University where he was buried at the grand age of 98 years. Initially educated at Dent Grammar School, he was no ordinary scientist being a pioneer in his field.

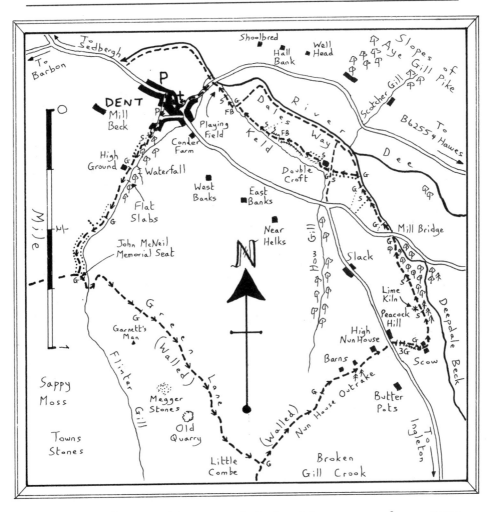

As you enter the church by its porch, look out for an unusual gravestone sporting a square notch. This is the final resting place of George Hodgson, who is said to have signed a pact with the Devil himself. A man of remarkably robust constitution until death claimed the old rascal in 1715, his fitness is laid at Old Nick's scheming door.

When local citizens met an untimely demise in mysterious circumstances, the blame was firmly attributed to George's restless spirit. It was decided, therefore, to unearth his remains and re-inter them near the porch, presumably to counter the Devil's malignant influence. The square notch is supposed to be where a stake was driven through his heart – one of the few methods of irrevocably despatching a vampire. Apparently it was the shape of George's teeth that led to him being labelled one of the 'undead'.

Returning to the car park along the cobbled main street, resist the temptation so early to sample Dent Brewery's "best beer under the sun". Bear left up the lane opposite, passing the vicarage on your right. Beyond a bend in the narrow lane, the paved route ends and the fell track begins.

Climbing quite steeply out of the valley, it enters tree cover beside Flinter Gill, kinking to the right to reach the first stile. The exceedingly stony track is unusual in that it has assiduously resisted the incessant pummelling from a myriad of booted pedestrians. Continue upwards where the gill has cut a deep cleft into the fellside.

As the ruin of High Ground is approached, watch for a plunging cataract on the far side. Beyond and above, the tumbling waters pour over a stepped link of gritstone slabs. Above the treeline, the gradient eases and the track becomes walled on both sides, eventually joining Green Lane at a gated T-junction. A seat dedicated to the memory of a local man by the name of John McNeil offers the chance to rest and admire the sweeping panorama along the length of Dentdale.

Head left along the walled track that was used at one time as a drove road for herds of Scottish cattle on their way to the meat-hungry markets of middle England. It makes a fine high-level route linking Barbon with Kingsdale, avoiding Dent altogether. Following a sharp zigzag to cross the upper reaches of Flinter Gill, the track straightens as it contours across this eastern flank of Great Coum Fell.

A series of prominent cairns on the near horizon are of prehistoric origin and known as the Meggar Stones. Stick with Green Lane until a major walled lane on the left is reached that will take you back down to valley level. Once High Nun House is passed, cross straight over Deepdale Lane through a trio of gates. Follow a fence on your right down to another gate above the abandoned farm of Scow.

Drop down between the old farmhouse and barn then swing sharp left towards a line of conifers beside Deepdale Beck. Accompany them to mount a wall stile with a limekiln at the far side. Keep this side of the continuing line of trees up to another stile slightly offset up the banking. After a further 100 metres, a yellow daub on the broken wall fronting the trees points the way down to the beck side and along to Mill Bridge.

Cross the valley road but not the bridge, continuing along the same side of the beck. We have now joined the celebrated Dales Way, which accompanies the River Dee all the way down the valley. After negotiating a small gate, the path swings sharp right, hemmed into the riverbank by a wire fence. Pass through a stile and two more gates before slanting left away from Deepdale Beck alongside a wall.

This deviation from the Dales Way avoids the more popular section before it merges once again on the approach to Dent. Cross straight over the track serving Double Croft to pass behind the farm buildings and so enter a passage at the far side by a wall stile. Squeezed between a wall and hedge for no more than 100 metres, the path thereafter accompanies a fence only on the left. Keep with this when it reverts to a hedge all the way round to a footbridge.

The route then follows a narrow rill known simply as Keld, a fence preventing ingress to the field pastures. Mount a stile in the fence. Opposite is a wall stile to continue alongside Keld, now joined by a parallel stream, the two merging as a field bridge is reached. When I last came this way, the wire fence had disintegrated leaving the wooden stile lonely and isolated (April 1999).

Use the footbridge to cross to the far side of Keld once again and join part of the Dales Way. Straddle a stile to enter a passage constricted between the beck and a substantial fence adjacent to the local playing field. On reaching the road, slant left back into Dent, passing through the churchyard for another look at that strange final resting place.

Judge for yourself whether the hole in George Hodgson's gravestone was hollowed out for a fence post as claimed by sceptics. Being an ardent fan of Christopher Lee, I much prefer the alternative explanation.

9. Rydale

No Longer at this Address

Mysteries: Carlow Stones, GR 921877; The Last Village, GR 920873

Distance Walked: 7 miles

Total Height Climbed: 900 feet, 274 metres

Start/Finish: After leaving Bainbridge, turn right up Blean Lane for 1½ miles. Parking is available on the grass verge immediately beyond the bridleway serving the farming settlement of Low Force.

Terrain: Rolling grass pastures in the valley surrender to the high-level limestone plateaux. A steep climb out of the valley is on indistinct grassy paths.

Map Required: Ordnance Survey 1:25000 Outdoor Leisure 30, Yorkshire Dales Northern & Central areas

One of those delectable side valleys tucked away out of sight, Rydale hangs above the ever-popular Wensleydale and is missed by those who have eyes only for the obvious. Such blinkered individuals inevitably miss the 'Jewel of the Dales' nestling in its glacial hollow. Surrounded by walled-in pastures that soar aloft to the circlet of limestone scars, Semerwater is second only in size to Malham Tarn and was probably much larger in days of yore when it stretch further up the dale.

From the mouth of the lake flows the shortest river in England. Unusual it certainly is in that the two-mile stretch begins in languid mood, the River Bain then plunging down a series of cataracts through the village below.

Our walk begins with a stroll down the access track serving Low Force but signposted to Low Blean, further up the valley towards Semerwater. Just before the track swings sharply to the left, cut back right down to a wall corner and a brief passage containing a gate. Then accompany the wall on your left in a due westerly direction across the flat valley floor. Pass through a gate at the end near to a stone barn. With a fence on the right, a walk of 200 metres will bring you to the next gate before another barn. Now make your way down to the riverbank, heading upstream over an intervening fence stile to reach the triple-arched road bridge.

Close by are the Carlow Stones, which are said to have been deposited there as a result of some devious contest between fallen angels. Eventually tiring of their lethal game, the devilish duo left the rocks where they had come to rest, neither having bested the other.

Perhaps this story from the 'nether world' had some influence on the

Does a shamed village lie beneath the placid calm of Semerwater?

ghostly meeting between a canny Dalesman and the mysterious Lady in Black. When this white-faced chimera failed to acknowledge his cheery "Goodnight", the farmer felt a decidedly odd sensation. A fellow traveller along the road to Stalling Busk who soon caught him up denied having witnessed anything unusual on the road that evening. An unnerving experience for the poor fellow, who was definitely not prone to flights of fantasy.

But on the fine sunny day that I arrived at the bridge, nothing so outlandish could besmirch the tranquil scene that unfolded across the placid reach of Semerwater. Looking out over this calm surface, speculation regarding the Iron Age village that once lined the shore flitted casually through my mind. When the level was lowered in 1937, flint spear and axe heads were discovered, proving the existence of the enigmatic settlement and possibly a castle prior to the flooding that devastated the wooden houses. How and why this occurred has been passed down through generations of Dales folk.

The most intriguing of the legends concerns the appearance of a poor traveller who found himself lost in Rydale one cold winter's night. Hungry and cold, his pleas for food and shelter were constantly rejected by the callous residents. Even the local priest refused him as mush as a drink of water. It was only when he climbed up the far side of the valley that a humble shepherd and his wife invited the beggar in to share their meagre lot. Next morning after breakfast, he bid them farewell and climbed the slopes of Addlebrough to observe the churlish settlement from on high. Raising his arms to the heavens, the man brought down a damning curse that was to seal the village's fate for all eternity:

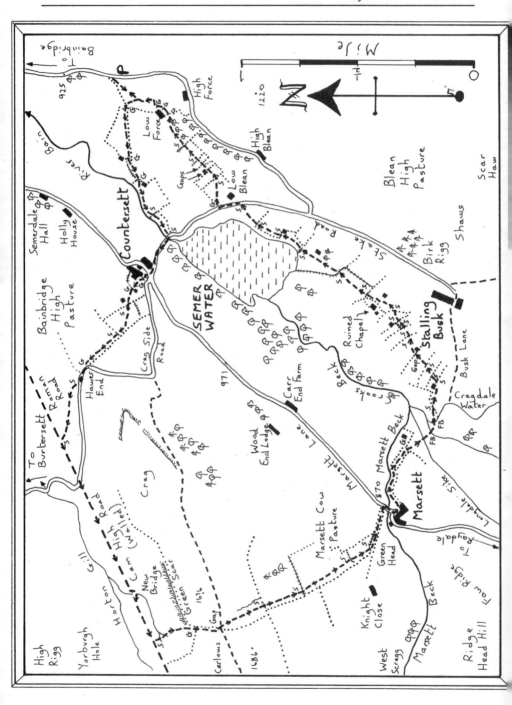

> *Semerwater rise! Semerwater sink!*
> *Swallow all the houses!*
> *But save the small house*
> *Where they gave me food and drink.*

Whereupon, dark clouds filled the sky at his bidding. Thunder, lightning, torrential rain and everything in between pummelled the hollow until the village finally disappeared, never to be resurrected. All that remained was the shepherd's cottage.

But what of the mysterious stranger? Some say he was an emissary sent from God to test the charity of a village where selfishness had become endemic. Following the village's demise, the avenging angel rose into the firmament having completed his master's behest. The more sensitive inhabitants of Rydale claim to have seen the tops of buildings and heard bells ringing – but only when night has fallen, naturally.

Cross the bridge and strike up the lane to reach Countersett. Should this walk be undertaken on August Bank Holiday Monday, you will be rewarded with a grandstand view of the service conducted by the Vicar of Askrigg from a boat on Semerwater. This tradition, instigated in 1956, helps to perpetuate the legend of the Lost Village.

Or maybe it is in memory of Humphrey Hopper, who used to swim across the lake everyday in all weathers. A renowned tall story teller, 'Aud Humph' often rowed visitors on the lake and claimed to have seen the village whilst diving into the murky depths for a lost penknife. Another of Humphrey's assertions was that he would rise from the grave and haunt those who had scoffed at his stories. Some of the more gullible inhabitants say they have seen the ghost of the crafty cove riding a white horse.

Upon reaching the crossroads, bear right towards Countersett then left down a track skirting the top end of the village. Immediately ahead is the old hall where Richard Robinson, the first Quaker in Wensleydale, lived in the 17th century. He was instrumental in establishing a strong following in the Dales. Even George Fox stayed here in 1677 before a permanent meeting house was built.

Go through a gate on the left and stride along the fence for 100 metres before forking left up the grass bank. Aim to the right of a prominent barn ahead, opening a gate to continue uphill. As it becomes increasingly steep, slant left to join a rising wall and another barn, beyond which is a wall stile.

Make a diagonal crossing of the next field on a grass path that takes advantage of a cutting to reach the wall stile above. Now accompany the wall on your left up to a gate and thus gain the fell road at Hawes End. Maintain a westerly course for 100 metres then lean right through a wall stile and half left down a shallow gradient. Make towards the white gate in the walled track known as Cam High Road.

Then it's left up the broad Roman road that connects the fort at Bainbridge with Ingleton. Many are the tramping legions that must have stamped their presence on this wild and bleak terrain in those far distant times. Much wider than originally planned, medieval cowboys herding their cattle to far-flung markets later used it as a drove road.

The only kink in the otherwise arrow-straight highway occurs at New Bridge where the infant Horton Gill cuts a notched path down the fellside. Stick with this road for a mile until a signposted stile to Marsett is reached. Cross a pair of shallow fords, aiming to the right of Green Scar where the path finds a gap across the plateau of Scar Hill. Beyond a gate, the route accompanies a broken wall to the far side of the open fell.

Pass through a gap in the wall, now on your right, and slant gradually away from it and down an increasingly steep gradient as the stepped valley falls away into Rydale. A faint path in the grass improves as height is lost, pursuing a direct course through four stiles to reach the enclosed track below serving Knight Close.

Bear left down to the road and right across the bridge into the farming hamlet of Marsett. Accompany a track round to the left, rejoining Marsett Beck for 200 metres before forking right along a short, walled corridor, gated at the end. The path then straddles two small becks by means of attendant footbridges. After the second of these, bear left along a wall and over a stile, chaperoning the wall, now on your left, up,to a barn. At the far side of this, our route follows a narrow but clear path heading north-east back towards Semerwater. Numerous walled enclosures are negotiated using stiles with small integral gates to contain the wandering woollies.

Notable along this section is the ruined chapel of Busk. Erected in 1722 on the site of a much older structure, the eye-catching display of stone archways effectively complements the adjacent graveyard, a most intriguing finale that man could never better. Further along the path nudges past the lake, now designated as a wildlife nature reserve affording a safe haven for plants and animals to flourish.

On reaching the valley road at Low Blean, the continuing right of way through the farmyard has become impassable (April 1999). Although still sanctioned by the authorities, the farmer has recognised this and is prepared to assist walkers by providing a diversion. So head left towards Countersett for 100 metres then go though a gate on the right to make a diagonal crossing of the field. Locate a wall stile to continue the walk down the valley. Pass through a gap beside a small stone building and through another soon after.

Maintain a north-easterly course through two stiles and along a thin line of trees on the approach to Low Force. Lean right through a gate and along a short track through two more gates to gain the access track back upto Blean Lane where the car is parked.

10. Bainbridge

Blow Your Own Trumpet

Mysteries: Hornblowers, GR 934903; The Lost Abbey, GR 937909
Distance Walked: 5 miles
Total Height Climbed: 350 feet, 107 metres
Start/Finish: Arriving at Bainbridge from the direction of Hawes, fork right up a lane beside the village green where ample parking is available.
Terrain: Rolling grass pastures separated by drystone walls, with rugged cliff scarring above the valley bottoms.
Nearest Shops: Askrigg
Map Required: Ordnance Survey 1:25000, Yorkshire Dales Northern and Central areas

One of a series of 'stony' villages lining either side of Wensleydale, Bainbridge is unique in a number of ways. Not least is the largest village green I have ever encountered. Cricket matches, fairs and sports events were regularly held on the green in days gone by, the latter now being held in a field near Yore Bridge on Spring Bank Holiday.

Then, of course, there is the choice site atop Brough Hill where the Romans elected to build a fort some years back. Numerous artefacts were uncovered when the site was excavated early in the 20th century. The latter stages of this walk offer the best view of the fort when its outer limit and entrance causeway can be picked out. From here, a splendid road was constructed over the fells to Ingleton, only occasionally deviating from a straight line.

In the Dark Ages, much of the valley was swathed in a green blanket of dense forest and Bainbridge became the centre for its management. The monarch regarded it as his own personal playground and hunted the wild beasts that also preyed on unwary travellers. Guides were employed to conduct parties through the suffocating expanse of greenery and a horn was blown at regular intervals to inform travellers of their location.

Everyone then knew they were approaching Bainbridge. The original bullock horn is now lodged in Bolton Castle, its successor being kept at the Rose and Crown Inn in the village. Presented to the hornblowers of Bainbridge in 1864, it came from an African water buffalo. People once set their watches by the horn before the days of radio and it could even be heard in distant Askrigg when the wind was right. Many of the hornblowers were

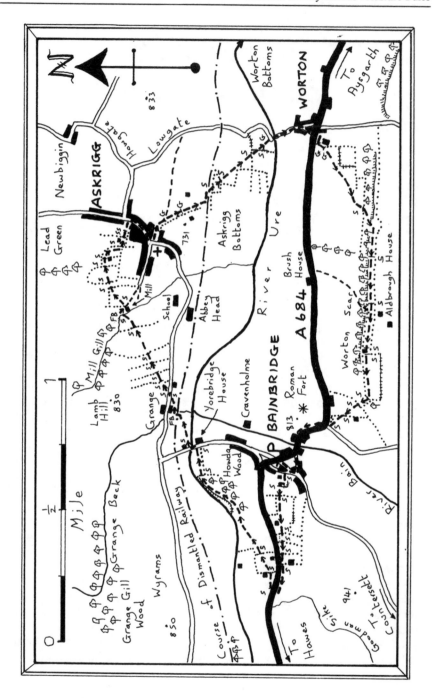

Metcalfes, who prided themselves on their punctuality, claiming never to have missed a blow.

On one occasion, Jamie Metcalfe was carousing in Askrigg when the church bell made him realise he was late for his appointed sound-off. Quickly returning to Bainbridge, he finally pumped out the regulation three blasts at 9.30pm. When his wife was informed, she immediately came back with the caustic retort, "They've had a double dose tonight then. Our George blew it at 9 o'clock."

But like many such quaint old customs, the blowing of the Bainbridge horn has become a spasmodic affair largely confined to special events. Could this be due to the removal of the forests for cultivation, the arrival of the digital wristwatch, or maybe even the Ordnance Survey and their invaluable maps? Time marches on and it is a futile effort to restrict progress.

Take advantage of a narrow ginnel to reach the upper lane, then heading left until you arrive at the village primary school. Sandwiched between it and the Wesleyan Chapel built in 1836 is a fenced passage that should be followed round the edge of the school grounds to a stile. Then cross a short field to the next stile in a wall. Maintain a due west direction over three more wall stiles before slanting right to the final one giving onto the main road.

Bear left, keeping to the grass verge on the opposite side for 200 metres in the direction of Hawes. Watch for a hidden wall stile down the banking. Turn back along the wall now on your right up to a stile adjoining a barn complete with sheep pens. Keep right of this through a gate to cross the next field, nudging a wall corner on the left. Drop down to the flats beside the River Ure, strolling on towards some trees lining the riverbank. Slant upward into the trees on a path that rises above the acclivitous gradient carved out by the river's outer edge. The path drops down to the river below a series of landslip buffers erected to prevent the trees disappearing into the waters.

Soon after, mount a stile and amble over to join the road opposite Yorebridge House. Now used as a centre for National Park activities, it used to be a prestigious school founded in 1601 by Anthony Besson. His aim was to improve education in the district, charging only according to a person's ability to pay, although some boys escaped payment altogether by carrying wood and water for the headmaster's house. Its solid reputation for academic excellence was tested in the mid-19th century when the incumbent teacher spent much of his time fishing. This was a mere blip in an otherwise unblemished record that is continued at the new school site near to Askrigg which opened its doors in 1931.

Cross the bridge then lean right through a stile adjoining a stone outbuilding to make your way over the field to its far corner. Go through the gap once spanned by the valley railway and over the single-file Bow Bridge, thought to have connections with the monks of Fors Abbey. Soon after our route crosses a track gated at either side as it forges onward behind the scattered dwellings that form the hamlet of Grange to reach the Askrigg road.

One of these buildings used to be known as Chantry Farm (now Abbey Cottage), where the remains of the 12th-century abbey can still be seen. Only the trefoiled window and flat-headed doorway remain, sufficient however to conjure up images of a monastic struggle with the harsh elements in what was then a wild and inhospitable environment.

Peter de Quincey strove hard to establish a colony in this part of Wensleydale for 11 years, but it was the Abbot of Savigny who finally terminated the project which he claimed would never succeed in such an austere location. Peter's entreaty to allow the settlement to continue fell on deaf ears and he was eventually forced to abandon the abbey following a series of bad harvests.

Disillusioned by their failure, the sad procession of monks made its way back to more accommodating terrain around Jervaulx Abbey. When the railway was built across the site, excavations revealed human bones presumably belonging to those monks for whom the exacting regime of Fors proved too much. It is not surprising, therefore, that the environs around the old abbey are haunted. Not by its ancient forebears as you might expect but by a little green man dressed in green. Now where has he originated?

Turn right away from this rather sad arena for 100 metres then take to the fields on the opposite side of the road through a stile. Head half right up rising ground in an east-north-east direction. Count off six more wall stiles, which should bring you to the enclosed cutting of Mill Gill. Cross the footbridge to swing immediately right then left under a metal duct carrying water to the old mill.

Beyond the next stile the slabbed path heaves right across the level field towards Askrigg. A more sporting alternative is to fork left up the pathless grass banking to the far left corner of the field. Following two stiles in rapid succession, stride over the next field to a stile at the far side. Continue onward with a wall on your left through a stile on the north side of a ruined barn. Then make a broad right-hand sweep down to a gap stile hidden until the last minute at the field corner.

Go through this to cross the adjacent field, keeping right of a large barn to gain the far side. Now accompany the wall backing onto the outer edge of Askrigg's built-up area along to an iron gate. Having arrived in a constricted passage, follow it round to reach the main street down a short flight of steps.

Bear right down to the heart of the village that was at one time the focus of life in Wensleydale. Innovation was amply demonstrated in the 18th century when the village became a renowned clockmaking centre with one of the craftsmen, Christopher Caygill, delighting in adorning his dials with pictures of the Devil. During the same period Askrigg produced scarves and other knitted garments made from 'cotton', although this particular mill soon changed to the established manufacture of woollen goods.

But when the turnpike road on the far side of the valley was engineered, Hawes grew to prominence leaving Askrigg to stagnate. Its fame was resurrected in the classic series "All Creatures Great and Small" when the vets' surgery was used for outside scenes opposite the market cross.

Take the lane opposite the cross between a scattering of cottages, soon leaning right into open country. The path drops down through a gate alongside a wall to cross the old railway line and the wall at the far side. Heading south-east in a straight line, the narrow slabbed pathway indicates that this was once an important link route between Askrigg and the far side of the valley. On reaching the River Ure, cross the bridge and go up the road on the far side into the village of Worton.

A poignant message for visitors to Worton

An amalgam of hoary old cottages that are missed by the motorist who sticks to the main road, Worton Hall on the right is reckoned to be the oldest habitation in the dale. Opposite a surviving red telephone box stands a cottage boasting the poignant epistle – "1729, Michael Smith, Mechanick. But He that built all things is God". Such an august title meant that Michael had quarried and transported all the stone for the building himself, and then set to work – a common enough undertaking in those days.

Clearly relying on his Maker for encouragement in the enterprise, we can but contemplate whether Michael would have sympathised or even been involved with the Bread Riot that took place here in 1757. The high price of corn had impoverished the Dales folk, who seized a supply of bread being delivered to some 'gentlemen' from Wharfedale. Several ringleaders were caught and arrested at Middleham Market for paying only what they wanted for the cornmeal. They ended up in Richmond Jail as a result of their futile protest.

Take a right along the main road towards Bainbridge for only 50 metres, crossing over to pass through the first gate. Stroll up to another on the right of a farm building ahead. Then lean half right across the rising field to nudge the corner of a fenced enclosure as you aim for the line of trees below Worton Scar. At the end of a broken wall, lean in to locate a wall stile at the edge of the trees.

A path climbs up through a breach in the cliff face. At the top, keep this side of the wall, heading west along the upper rim of the Scar. After the second stile the path enters a wide corridor at the end of which are two stiles close together abutting a hut. Entering the open field beyond, stick with the wall on the right to its far corner, passing through a stile to head downhill towards Bainbridge in the valley below.

This is the best position from which to observe the raised dais where the Romans chose to erect their fort. A splendid site to oversee the dale in all directions. Maintaining a north-westerly course through a trio of stiles will bring you to the Semerwater road and its junction with the A684. Continue down the road to cross the River Bain and so return to the village.

This carved seat adds character to the woodland trail near Aysgarth Falls (Walk 11)

11. Aysgarth
Prisoner Royal

Mystery: Castle Bolton, GR 034918

Distance Walked: 7½ miles

Total Height Climbed: 400 feet, 122 metres

Start/Finish: Make use of the official car park adjoining the National Park information centre, which occupies the old buildings of Aysgarth Railway Station. If this is full or closed, take advantage of a pull-in beside the A684 to the west of the Palmer Flatt Hotel. This will involve an extra quarter mile of road walking at the start and end of the walk.

Terrain: Enclosed meadows rise gradually out of the valley bottom to merge with rough grazing on the higher ground. Clear paths most of the way.

Nearest Shops: Aysgarth

Map Required: Ordnance Survey 1:25000 Outdoor Leisure 30, Yorkshire Dales Northern & Central areas

The name of Aysgarth has become famous for the spectacular waterfall display tucked away in the valley bottom, removed from the main flow of traffic along Wensleydale. Aysgarth village, an attractive settlement in its own right, remains aloof from the awesome phenomenon that has brought national recognition and set it apart from other Dales villages. Only two other natural features synonymous with the Dales limestone terrain attract similar multitudes, and they are at Ingleton and Malham.

Within the short space of half a mile, the River Ure at Aysgarth plunges headlong over a trio of stepped cataracts, all of which can be safely viewed on the woodland trail alongside the river. Here the Ure has chiselled out a course to accommodate the glacially over-deepened side valley of Bishopdale. One of a rare handful of bridging points in Wensleydale, a steep and twisting descent is necessary from the main road at Palmer Flatt. The bridge was widened in 1788 to accommodate the increased traffic occasioned by the flour mill, which took full advantage of the swift surge to increase its output of cornmeal.

However, not everybody was well disposed to this harnessing of the river for industrial purposes. Even the advent of the railway era was fervently resisted for a time until the inevitable hand of progress overruled all resistance. One correspondent described it as, "a great flouring mill whose stream has drawn off half the water of the falls...all the valley is disturbed...rebellion may be near at hand." Such were the sentiments of a time when rapid industrial change both in town and country was regarded by many as a threat to a way of life unchanged for centuries.

Following a turbulent past, the building now houses a museum of horse-drawn carriages; and the Ure rushes by unhindered once again. Hemmed in by tree-lined bankings, the turbid flow rumbles and roars like an express train powering through the gorge in unrestrained fury. It is truly an inspiring place from which to commence our walk.

Stroll up the road towards Carperby for 200 metres then branch right through a gate into Freeholders' Wood. Now owned by the Dales National Park, freeholders from Carperby still retain the right to gather wood by means of hazel coppicing. This involves trimming back the shoots at ground level to encourage new growth that is ready for cutting in a few years – unlike mature trees that take considerably longer to grow.

Almost immediately a flight of stone steps on the right lead down to the fenced platform which affords the finest of viewpoints for the Middle Force. Returning to the main path, continue east through the woods to emerge by a gate. Keep alongside a fence on your right until the next gate, which takes you back into the wooded fringe of the riverbank. Drop down the narrow trail then swing right to the next observation platform close to Lower Force.

After this final display of extrovert exhibitionism, continue downstream for 100 metres to mount a fence stile. Strike up the grassy bank away from the river to meet a fence. Bend right along this to a stile then make a beeline for Hollins House up an easy gradient intermittently sprinkled with trees. Go through a gate, followed soon after by the farmyard. Keep left of the house and leave by the access track.

When it veers to the left, fork away right along a grass track across open ground. Adjacent to a small copse, slip round an isolated gate and onward to the

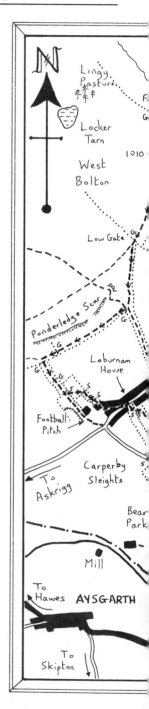

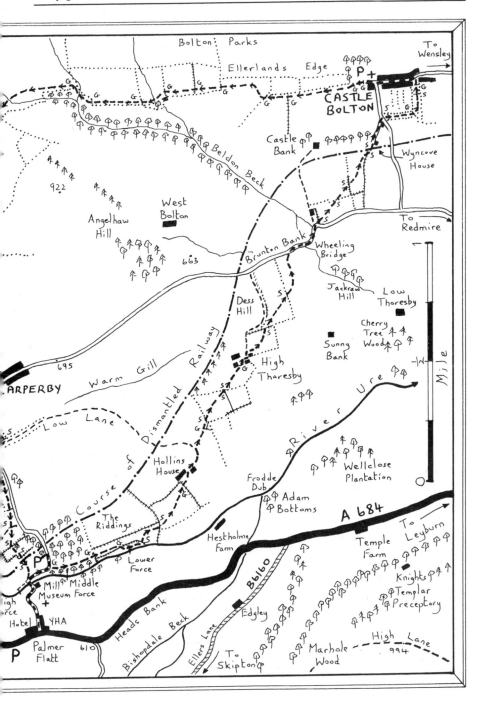

wall ahead. Straddle the stile to make a diagonal crossing of the meadow to its far corner where a pair of stiles will bring you into the next field. Maintain the same direction to reach High Thoresby. In front, the sturdy grey fortress of Bolton Castle dominates the view, imposing its primeval bearing on the entire valley hereabouts.

The village of Thoresby dates from the time when the Danish chieftain Thor settled here. It disappeared from the valley during the 14th century, some say due to the ravages of the plague, which wiped out the entire village community. A smattering of low hummocks can still be traced, marking the building foundations of this vanished settlement.

What is impossible for us to ignore is the mighty blockhouse ahead that makes a fitting objective to aim for. A gate followed by a stile will find you approaching a lone barn to the right of the main farm. Go through the adjacent gate and lean right off the access track to cross a field, at the far side of which a fence stile should be straddled. Then lean right over this field to leap a stile halfway along the facing wall. Join the Sunny Bank access track to reach the road from Carperby at Brunton Bank.

Head right along the road for a quarter of a mile, leaving at a sharp right-hander. Mount a fence stile on the far side to diagonally cross the field and a wall stile at the opposite side. This is followed soon after by another, after which you should walk towards the right boundary of the treeline ahead. At the top right corner of the field, climb a stile then another to cross the course of the old railway.

Pass left of Wyncove House to accompany the paved access road until it joins the road up to Castle Bolton. Cross straight over to follow an old walled track until a gate is reached. Then swing left and over to the opposite wall of a narrow field which will lead you unerringly to the village's one and only street.

Turn left down towards the castle along the concourse with its broad grass verge. The stone cottages are completely overshadowed by the towering bulwark of Bolton Castle. Confusion often arises with the 'turnabout' name of village and castle. Nor should it be mistaken for Bolton Abbey or Bolton Priory, both separate entities in their own localities.

Strolling down the street, the cubist proportions of this awesome redoubt attack the senses in no uncertain manner. Much older than the accompanying village, the castle was constructed by the first Richard de Scrope in the 14th century. It was regarded as "a climax of English military architecture", creating an orderly balance between defence, domestic need and comfort.

Staunch upholders of the Catholic faith, the Scropes earned a steadfast reputation for honesty and fair dealing, trusted even by the Protestant ruling class. So when Elizabeth I decided to incarcerate Mary Queen of Scots to forestall any threat to her throne, it was to Bolton Castle and the Scropes that she turned. Today the castle remains the only property in England still existing where Mary was held captive.

Back in July of 1568, Mary's situation at Bolton Castle was far from uncomfortable and she is alleged to have employed more staff than the entire garrison, many of whom were boarded out at local farms. Certainly she was able to enjoy a life of relative luxury, albeit under the close supervision of her guardians. More a fortified house than a traditional castle, it amply suited Mary's regal status even though she was allowed little freedom of movement. Her quarters were in the south-west tower, from where a daring escape took place with the aid of young Kit Norton from Rylstone (See Walk 27). Climbing out of an unguarded window, this unlikely duo headed for Leyburn along a route known as The Shawl.

All too soon, however, they heard the yelp of baying hounds and the pounding of hooves from pursuers now hot on the trail of the fugitives. In her haste, Mary's wrap was snagged on a thorn bush and snatched from her shoulder. The pair had little chance of evading the pursuit and were captured within two hours at a spot that became known as 'The Queen's Gate'. That section of the fellside later adopted the title of Leyburn Shawl. Mary was returned to Bolton Castle under armed escort whilst Kit paid the supreme penalty, charged with high treason against the Crown. But for two hours at least, Mary tasted freedom with a man who clearly loved her for herself and not merely for the privilege of her regal position.

Ghostly sightings of the captive queen have been reported on numerous occasions. Was that really Mary Queen of Scots perceived walking along the crumbling battlements or merely a shadow thrown upon the cloudy backdrop? The stories abound, particularly in the vicinity of Nappa Hall, five miles to the west, where Mary spent two nights during a hunting trip, under supervision naturally.

This enigmatic pretender to the English throne was finally removed from Bolton Castle in January 1569 after only a six-month stay. In the following century, the country was plagued by civil war and the castle authorities came down on the side of Charles I and the Royalist cause. Held under siege by parliamentary forces in 1645, the garrison was reduced to eating horseflesh. Cromwell attempted to destroy Bolton Castle in 1647, without much success as we can see on the approach to what remains of this stout-hearted structure.

Admire the pitted remnants of the castle as you pass between it and St Oswald's Church. Beyond the car park, accompany the broad field track heading due west to contour this gently shelving flank of Wensleydale. After passing through nine gates, the path leans right to ford the upper reaches of Beldon Beck, wooded throughout much of its length. Soon after we pass through another gate, the path now indistinct as it bears left to follow a wall.

When the wall shoots off into the cutting below left, stick with the rim before descending to ford the beck. Another 150 metres will bring you to the wall enclosing the extensive upland grazing of Bolton West Park. Go through the gate, bearing half left along a flattened grass causeway now heading south. After a half mile beyond Low Gate, fork left down a steepening gradient alongside a wall. At the bottom of Ponderledge Scar the path merges with a fell track known as Peatmoor Lane that once served the lead mines high on Carperby Moor. Cross over this track through a gate to follow the lower edge of the scar alongside the wall on your left.

Once a gate has been negotiated, stroll on for another 100 metres, keeping an eye open for the broad-walled corridor leading down into Carperby village. Bear left through a gate and down the track until a sharp dip is reached just before the football field then slip through a stile in the wall on your left and over to another at the far side of the adjacent meadow.

Here another walled passage is entered. Beyond the next stile below, the right of way goes between farm buildings – notably remembered when I passed this way for the ferocity of the dog population. Luckily they were chained up so any caustic remarks could be returned with impunity, trusting the chains to hold firm. Cross the farm access road and continue to a house, bending right then left to reach the village main street. Its market cross was erected in 1674 where the Quaker leader George Fox once preached beside it.

Take a right down a passage signposted to Aysgarth alongside Laburnum House. Mount a stile at the end and lean immediately left over another into the adjoining field. Follow the wall on the left edge down to Low Lane, the service road for Hollins House. Now head right then left towards Aysgarth for 50 metres only. Leap a stile on the right and follow the road inside the field down to a stile at the end. The path now forks away from the road to cross an old abandoned track that once served Bear Park. Keep right of a small clutch of fenced trees to mount a stile and continue down an easy gradient to negotiate another, after which the woodland fringe is reached.

Slide over the embankment of the old railway track and so return to the falls car park. If you have elected to park elsewhere, continue along a fenced pathway down to the bridge, retracing your steps up the far side of the valley.

12. West Witton
Head for the Hills

Mysteries: The Burning of Old Bartle, GR 061884; Penhill's Giant, GR 055867; Knights' Chapel, GR 036888
Distance Walked: 7½ miles
Total Height Climbed: 1150 feet, 351 metres
Start/Finish: Pull off the A684 at Swinithwaite, where the village green abuts directly onto this busy main road through Wensleydale.
Terrain: Rising enclosed pastures surrender to the rough moorland of Penhill with its north-facing gritstone cliffs.
Nearest Shops: West Witton
Map Required: Ordnance Survey 1:25000 Outdoor Leisure 30, Yorkshire Dales Northern & Central areas

Impossible to ignore, Penhill occupies a vast wedge of bleak terrain between Wensleydale and Coverdale. Its flanks are dotted with the relics of bygone ages when superstition and ignorance ruled man's conception of his life on earth. A beacon that once warned of impending danger proudly announces the fell's importance for communications, being a vital link in the national chain that covered the country aeons before the advent of the internet revolution.

The name of Penhill itself is an Old English misnomer literally meaning 'hill-hill', for mountain it certainly is not – falling well short of the magical 2000ft contour. Low cliffs of exposed gritstone provide a stepped topography with walled terracing on each level down to the valley floor. Flat and featureless apart from the beacon on the edge of its eastern shoulder, Penhill nonetheless can claim an enviable pedigree draped in the hazy pall of an obscure yet fascinating past. Fell wanderers can enjoy peace and tranquillity; remote from the throbbing bustle that enfolds Hawes and Askrigg. So it will come as no surprise to learn that a nasty giant once dwelt up here, but more of this reviled character anon.

First set off up the narrow lane from Swinithwaite, climbing out of the valley until a thin belt of trees is passed. Go through the gate on your left to follow the walled upper edge of the treeline over three stiles until the path closes with the main road. Then lean right up a grass bank to a wall stile, followed soon after by a gate.

Now make a diagonal crossing of the next field to the far right corner, where a stile gives access to a pinched culvert at the edge of a small wood. Somewhat overgrown with thistles, this section is soon cleared by a stile at the far end. Halfway along the continuing wall, slip through a gap stile and along the opposite side to a fence stile at the end of the field. Maintain a straight line to reach the main road at the top of Mesnes Lane.

Bear right into West Witton. An elongated village straddling the main road, it has become well known far beyond the Dales for the ancient custom of 'Burning Old Bartle'. Thought by some to have a sinister connection with Saint Bartholomew, to whom the parish church is dedicated, the ceremony is far more likely to have its origins in pagan beliefs. Certainly the two contrasting feasts are celebrated on the same day, which is 24 August, but the ritual burning of the church's benefactor would not be condoned, even by today's liberal-minded society. My own preference leans towards 'Baal' – thought to be the Giant of Penhill and relative of the Norse god Thor. And when the story finally unfolds, I feel certain you will agree.

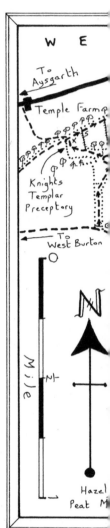

Processing along the main street of West Witton accompanied by much merriment and frequent calls for liquid refreshment at the hostelries, the effigy of 'Old Bartle' is burnt with a last rendering of the immortal ditty:

> *'In Penhill Crags he tore his rags,*
> *At Hunters Thorn he blew his horn,*
> *At Capplebank Stee he brake his knee,*
> *At Grisgill Beck he brake his neck,*
> *At Wadham's End he couldn't fend,*
> *At Grisgill End he made his end.'*

Should you wish to join in the celebration, then August 24 is the day to be reserved for this walk. Take the public footpath opposite the Wensleydale Heifer Inn, which leads from a small green into a narrow, walled alley zigzagging behind the houses to deposit you in the field at the rear. Slant half left to a stile, aiming for another across the next field.

Instead of mounting this one, strike up an easy slope beside the hedge towards the trees above. Go through a wall gap, veering right up a clear path to reach the upper limit, where the left of two stiles is chosen. Proceed along an intermittent line of trees until you reach the start of a walled track. Heading left along here will bring you to the Melmerby road. A stiled footpath parallels the track on the far side of the right-hand wall for use when heavy rain makes this route impassable.

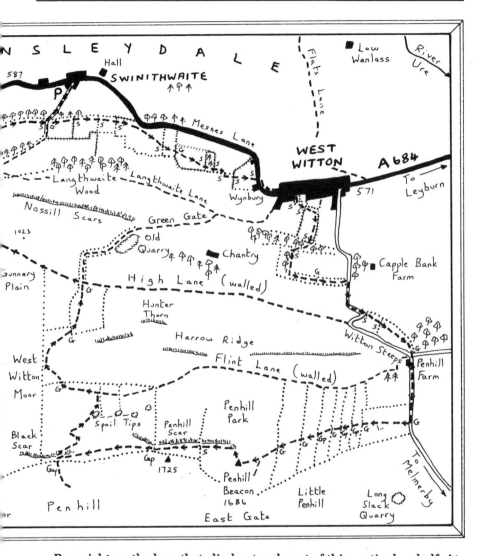

Bear right up the lane that climbs steeply out of this particular shelf. At the first sharp right, keep ahead through a stile followed soon after by another. Climbing steadily, the road above Witton Steeps is reached through a gate close to Penhill Farm.

Walk south up the road past the farm for 600 metres until a gate on the right indicates access to the moors. Pathless initially, head due west, keeping right of a piece of isolated walling to reach the next gate at the far end of this field. Strengthening thereafter, you will negotiate six wall barriers before gaining the open fell.

The beacon is clearly in view all the way and reached by a direct climb up this acclivitous shoulder of Penhill which forks right off the bridleway. Once a castellated tower, the current edifice is a substantial if rather sad cluster of stones that would appear to have replaced the original beacon site located 100 metres to the north. Views are especially extensive to the east, across a patchwork quilt of rustic charm.

Legend purports that the giant previously alluded to once lived up here in a mighty castle, his sole companion being a fierce dog named Wolfhead. His prize possession was a large herd of pigs, which he allowed to forage on the moor. Cruelty was etched deep into every crevice of the fellow's loathsome visage, often surfacing if one of his pigs was harmed. Strutting across the valley, he would often cause havoc amongst his farming tenants, who cowered in fear at his approach. One such occasion resulted in a local shepherd girl named Gunda being savagely attacked by the dog. When she retaliated, the giant picked up a large tree trunk and clubbed her to death. Although incensed by this act of wanton sadism, the Dales folk could only mourn their deceased, offering no resistance to the giant's abhorrent deeds.

Only when one of the giant's prize boars was mysteriously slain did he finally receive his just desserts. Summoning the villagers to his castle, he demanded to know who the guilty party was; threatening that all their children would be likewise terminated if the culprit was not exposed. The renowned Seer of Carperby, a wise old man possessing spiritual powers, warned the giant that if he persisted in carrying out his threat, he would never again enter his castle.

Next morning, the callous rogue left the castle and strode to the cliffs on Penhill to confront the fearful gathering. But on the way, he came upon many dead boars strewn across the moorland and was determined to show no mercy. Disregarding the Seer's caveat, the giant threatened all present with the direst retribution, only to find the tables well and truly turned.

Flames leapt from the castle ramparts as it was consumed in a rampant conflagration. Transfixed with shock, the giant began to tremble and quiver, for there, framed in the orange flames, was the ghost of the murdered Gunda. He staggered back in terror at this spectral manifestation and plunged over the edge of Penhill Crags to his death. And the people of Wensleydale were finally released from the despicable landlord forever.

From that very spot, a thin trod follows the rim of the abrupt downfall. Mount a stile at the wall end, continuing along the upper lip of Penhill Scar. A wall parallels the route set back on the left, with a trig column peeping out on the far side as the highest point is passed. Soon after, slide through a fence gap, keeping to the right of the wall for a further half a mile until a major gap is reached.

Take a right here down a clear trail that slants down this steep, rocky facade of Black Scar. The track makes a distinct zigzag part way down, eventually arriving at a spoil tip, one of a line at the base of the scars. Circle round the tip to follow a broken wall across this flat, reedy terrace until a major path is reached just beyond a metal water trough. Head left, forking towards a wall and gate.

Now slant half left to join a wall, following it down the next dip where the path leans right to reach a wall gate below. Pass through, continuing down an easier slope to arrive at High Lane by another gate. Bear left along this higher level walled track that provides access to numerous strip fields on this step of the terrace.

The monument on Penhill where a giant once roamed

After half a mile, heave right through a gate down a link track also walled for an initial 200 metres. It then forks right with the wall on the right as yet another steep section arrives. At the sharp hairpin, plough ahead between two stands of trees down to a gate at the end of the lower wood (to which English Heritage have granted access). Then amble across the field to the far corner where the fenced remains of a medieval chapel have been excavated.

The incumbent of Swinithwaite Hall discovered this small preceptory, together with residential quarters that still remain unexposed, in 1840. Bits of armour, spurs and horse accoutrements were also discovered at the same time. It was originally granted to the Knights Templar who owned much property in the valley in 1200 to "maintain a light perpetually burning in the chapel of Penhil". Dedicated to St Catherine, patron saint of linen weavers, the product that was worn by the Templars, the adjoining hospice offered shelter to passing travellers.

Not given to an excess of piety, the Templars lost control of the chapel and other lands hereabouts following a purge of their ranks in 1312. It was then handed over to the more 'respectable' Hospitallers. Head east along what must have been an important route in medieval times for half a mile. The path keeps to the upper edge of Long Back Wood, negotiating three stiles to reach the outward track. Bear left down this back to Swinithwaite.

13. Ingleton

Going Bats at Ribblehead

Mysteries: Batty Green, GR 764794; The Blue Clay Ghost, GR 758808

Distance Walked: 8 miles

Total Height Climbed: 1450 feet, 442 metres

Start/Finish: Approaching Ribblehead from the direction of Ingleton, turn left after the Station Inn and the cattle grid into a small car park. Many other pull-ins are available in the vicinity if this proves to be full.

Terrain: Rough moorland country comprising tussocky grass, initially on limestone, and with clear paths above the intake walls. Many stretches have been renovated due to severe erosion.

Nearest Shops: Ingleton

Map Required: Ordnance Survey 1:25000 Outdoor Leisure 2, Yorkshire Dales Southern and Western areas

It was once said that, "All the winds are at home at Ribblehead". On most of my previous visits, this declaration was indeed the case. But on the day of this particular walk, nothing could have been further from the truth. A golden orb beat down in unrestrained splendour from the cloudless sky painted a fine pastel blue from wall to wall. Complemented by a light breeze, the ascent of Whernside by the back door of Blea Moor was the perfect outing.

And when choosing to make the ascent of the Dales' highest mountain on such a day, nobody can complain if a host of other similarly minded individuals decide likewise. After all, they might well be toting this august volume – and who can blame them for that, certainly not I.

It has to be said that on most days a chill wind does indeed blast across the exposed moorland of Upper Ribblesdale, howling like a rabid banshee around the twenty-four arches that span the valley at this most renowned locale. It is, however, best to avoid 'Steam Special' days when the whole area is awash with trainspotters, photographers and rail enthusiasts of all descriptions.

Arguably the most scenic length of railway in the country heads north between Settle and Carlisle, making full use of this most famous of viaducts. Being close to the Ingleton-Hawes road ensures that even the most car-bound visitor is able to enjoy the full spectacle of this engineering phe-

Batty Green, where navvies laboured to build the celebrated Ribblehead Viaduct

nomenon in all its glory. Yet in spite of the distinction in which it now basks, the line was originally built out of desperation.

The Midland Railway in the 1860s wanted a Scottish link clear of its rivals on each of the coastal routes. It did, however, prove to be a costly investment, due in no small measure to the bleak terrain through which it ran. Decline of the local population followed later by the motorway network heralded its closure, even though it had survived the 'Beeching Axe' of the early 1960s. Thankfully this cloud hanging over the line's continuation has now been permanently consigned to an appropriate dustbin and its future as a major item of Dales railway heritage seems assured.

Stroll along the track from the Station Inn and as you approach the viaduct, consider the huge amount of labour and materials that went into its construction. This whole area known as Batty Green became a real life Wild West frontier town from 1869, boasting saloons, carpetbaggers, doss houses and a red-light district. It even had a hospital to contain the outbreak of smallpox that threatened to wipe out the entire workforce at one stage. Many of those who died are buried in the cemetery of the small church at Chapel-le-Dale where a memorial plaque inside commemorates their endeavours.

Every night when work had finished, the shanty town became a rip-roaring Hell's Kitchen. None of the disjointed array of tents and wooden shacks attained any degree of permanency, being thrown up with no thought for the future. The mossland would have been churned up into a sea of mud during the frequent downpours that occur in this part of the world. And like all temporary settlements, it soon disappeared into oblivion once the work was completed and the gangs of navvies moved on to the next section. A strange atmosphere does, however, linger to strike fear and trepidation into the hearts and minds of those who wander abroad over Batty Green even today. More especially when a dank curtain of grey smothers the moor in its fetid embrace. Strange events did inevitably linger in the mind of those who came after the navvies had departed.

When the shanty town was being dismantled, a frightening experience occurred in the hospital where a gruesome noise appeared to emanate from a coffin used for carrying the dead. Following a careful and tremulous investigation, it merely proved to be a drunk sleeping off the previous night's excesses. It was pointed out to the groggy inebriate that he could easily have been buried alive, whereupon he asked for the price of another drink before heading back to his home in Keighley.

Batty Wife Cave remains the most notable feature at the side of the road near the cattle grid. Now filled in, it was once a hole containing water at the time the railway was built. The story is told of a bickering couple who argued constantly before agreeing to separate. A reconciliation later ensued and a meeting at the hole was instigated. At first only the wife turned up and, thinking that she had been forsaken, immediately threw herself into the hole and drowned. When Mr Batty finally arrived, so distraught was he on learning of his wife's fate that he also made the ultimate sacrifice. The ghostly presence of this sad couple is reputed to haunt the environs of the cave, hoping to rekindle a love so abruptly terminated.

As you approach the viaduct, leave the main track to follow a grassy concourse up a re-laid section along the side of the railway heading north towards Blea Moor. Stick with this clear path over a stile to arrive at the signal box adjacent to an abandoned cottage. The box is permanently manned, the signal operator making use of the last train of the day to return home.

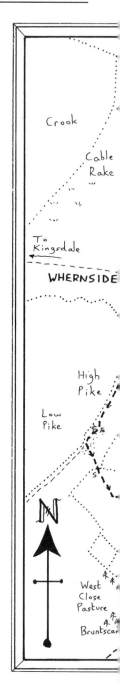

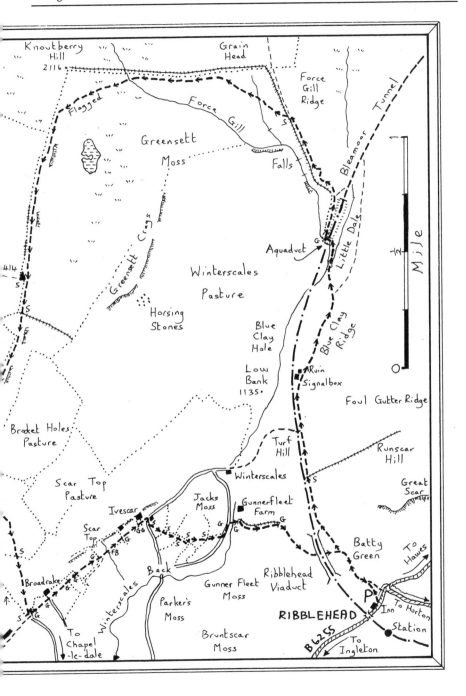

On a fine day with sunlight glinting off the silvery track, a more pleasant occupation is difficult to imagine. But when snow and violent gales lash this lonely moorland retreat, every creak and groan of the flimsy structure assumes a sinister intent, making one feel maybe that warm office in downtown Bradford isn't so dull after all.

Winter is the prime season for ghostly apparitions to make their presence felt along this outlying trail. One signalman recounted an incident when he was following a stranger who continued past the box on a particularly grim day, crossing the railway and disappearing into the blanched wilderness of Blea Moor. He thought nothing of the encounter until the frightful realisation struck home that the mysterious traveller had left no footprints in the snow.

Beyond the signal box, the path leans away from the chaperoning presence of the railway for the next mile to a stone footbridge. This major crossing point also acts as the aqueduct carrying Force Gill over the railway, which disappears into the bowels of Blea Moor 200 metres beyond. From above, the course of the underground line can be traced by means of the airshafts placed at regular intervals until it emerges in Dentdale.

After crossing the bridge, stick with the track that now slants away from the railway up the steepening shoulder of Force Gill Ridge. Accompany the fence on your left until a stile is reached where we take the more prominent path signposted to Whernside, here branching off the Craven Way. Follow this path across tussocky moorland to the wall/fence on Grain Head, thereafter leaning west until a flagged section forks left, climbing steadily up to the ridge ahead on the near horizon.

Head south up the gently shelving ridge beside the wall that runs virtually the entire length of the fell down to Ingleton Falls. Below left is Greensett Tarn nestling in a sea of tough sedges and marshland. From above it looks far prettier than is the case underfoot. As the summit arena is reached, a kink in the wall containing a gap stile enables the trig column to be visited on the far side.

The western prospect across Kingsdale to the Gregareth ridge is completely overshadowed by that encompassing this upper level of the Doe Valley towards Ingleborough's geometric profile. Highest point of the acclaimed 'Three Peaks Walk', Whernside is generally achieved by a direct assault from Winterscales by way of the fence that is encountered 200 metres beyond the summit.

Time constraints mean that walkers need to complete the designated 25-mile circuit, which also takes in Ingleborough and Penyghent, in less than twelve hours, a challenge accepted by thousands every year. Such is the popularity of the route that the erosion caused by overuse is a problem that the National Park authorities need to constantly monitor. First initiated by a duo of teachers from Giggleswick School back in 1887, they began at Horton-in-Ribblesdale and completed the circuit after classes had finished for the day. My own one-off attempt starting from Ribblehead failed to meet the deadline by an hour but it was an achievement to be savoured nonetheless.

At the base of Low Pike, our route bends down the steep escarpment to the intake wall. Mount one of a pair of ladder stiles and continue down in a south-westerly direction with one abrupt kink before reaching another wall stile. The gradient eases substantially down to the last stile that brings us to a low rim of limestone scarring bedecked with an array of trees.

Here we join the thoroughfare that once linked the settlements along The Scar with Ingleton and Dent. It now affords a route of distinction for walkers returning to Ribblehead. So progress left through the gate and on to the next one, thence passing Broadrake en route to a third and fourth close together. A 200-metre stroll across this field, maintaining a north-easterly course, will take you to yet another gate.

Our indistinct path then merges with a field track to cross a log bridge and so on to the next gate. Once the bungalow on the left is passed, a double gate enables you to negotiate the farmyard of Ivescar. Then head right down the access road, straddling the stile on your left immediately after the first modern barn.

Heading south-east, our primary aim now is to cross the enclosed valley pastures serving this isolated farming community. At the far side of the field, mount a stile to crest a low rise over Lockdiddy Hill, dropping down to another at the bottom. A further 50 metres will bring you to a stile on the left and deposit you in the adjacent field.

Lean half right to make a diagonal traverse through intermittent reed beds to reach a stile at the far side. Then keep to the wall on your left to gain the paved road heading left towards Winterscales Farm. Immediately beyond the first gate, swing hard right over the bridge spanning Winterscales Beck and another gate. Ignore the track upto Gunnerfleet, continuing onward on a clear track that leads unerringly back to Ribblehead. After passing beneath one of the soaring arches in the viaduct, pay a visit to the stone memorial erected to the memory of those hardy souls who provided unremitting labour to furnish such a splendid feat of engineering.

14. Hawes

Right Gear?

Mysteries: Gearstones, GR 780800; Lile Hob, GR 785803
Distance Walked: 5½ miles
Total Height Climbed: 650 feet, 198 metres
Start/Finish: Ample roadside parking is available along the B6255, on the right approaching Gearstones Lodge from the direction of Ribblehead. Alternatively, carry on for a quarter mile and park on the left, 100 metres before the sharp bend where our walk leaves the road.
Terrain: Wild and lonely moorland swathed in tough reeds and grass. Low hillocks interspersed with the occasional wall smother any notable landmarks. Straying from the established rights of way in this sprawling wilderness is consequently not recommended.
Nearest Shops: Hawes
Map Required: Ordnance Survey 1:25000 Outdoor Leisure 2, Yorkshire Dales Southern & Western areas

Since time immemorial the route between Ingleton and Hawes has provided a vital link connecting west and east of the country. Gently graded throughout, the Romans were the first to recognise this strategic lie of the land. Marching legions set out from the fort at Bainbridge following the natural Roman instinct to pursue the most direct course. Deviating from a straight line only to avoid major obstacles, the road merges with the current B6255 at the point where our walk properly begins.

Troops would have passed the spot where Gearstones now stands, over terrain unhindered by any stone walls or fencing. And as the jutting prow of Ingleborough reared out of the limestone bedrock, doubtless their thoughts centred on how best to eject the stubborn Brigantes from their mountain stronghold.

Once a public house, Gearstones was denigrated by Lord Torrington in 1792 as a "seat of misery, in a desert". Catering mainly for the needs of passing cattle drovers, it was rarely used by the gentry of the time who preferred the more civilising influence of urban locales. A twice-yearly agricultural fair in Upper Ribblesdale brought all manner of rustic traders to the inn, where copious barrels of ale slid down thirsty gullets with the ease of a well-oiled hiking boot.

Arrival of the railway across Ribblehead Viaduct and the new Station

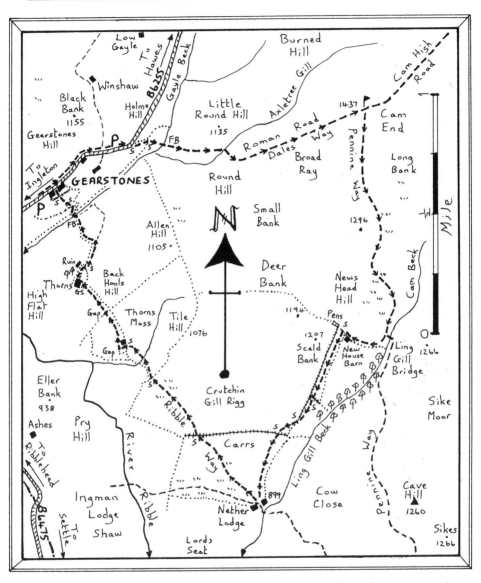

Inn sealed the fate of Gearstones as a public house. Thereafter, it was utilised as a lodge for entertaining the hunting fraternity. Up until the early
years of the 20th century, grouse shooting on the heather moors was a regular event starting on the 'glorious 12th' of August and culminating in the
Gearstones Ball held at the lodge in December.

Gearstones now dispenses educational advice rather than alcoholic beverages

Barrels of beer were brought over from Ribblehead to keep the gamekeepers and their beaters happy; whilst the elite of society no doubt supped champagne from fluted goblets. Certainly there was no shortage of men willing to beat the heather moors, the pay being much higher than they could earn as labourers. Most shoots lasted only four days then it was back to the daily grind on the farms.

Today Gearstones is still a lodge but run by the education authority as a field study centre. Walk past the old farmhouse and lodge for a quarter mile until you reach the brow of a rise followed by a sharp bend in the road. This is the point where we leave the road to begin the walk proper. It is also a likely spot where a boggle known as 'Lile Hob' would lie in wait for passing carts on their way up the valley.

This crafty cove was a domestic fairy generally thought to be helpful, although such denizens could cause mischief and annoy people with their devious pranks. When this was the case, a reading from the Bible together with the sticking of pins in a candle was said to result in their disappearance. This particular spectre vanished forever when a Dent shepherd by the name of Jack Sunter claimed that he had seen three silver rings poking out of the moss. Twirling them on a stick, one flew off and was lost for good, but the others were sold at Kirkby Lonsdale. Their removal from the moor effectively terminated the hitch-hiking exploits of 'Lile Hob' who was never seen again. Readers are invited to consider the origins of this strange and bewitching legend and what it all means. Answers on a postcard only.

Mount the ladder stile and descend a clear track alongside a wall to another at valley level. Cross the flood plain to squeeze along the plank footbridge for the walk up the old Roman highway. Climbing across this bleak wilderness on an easy gradient much favoured by Roman engineers, a silence you can almost hear settles over the featureless terrain.

And if a damp mist should seep into every nook and cranny of the moor, your isolation will be complete. That is until a group of trail bikers disturbs the ozone, the roar of throaty exhausts burning a hole in the blank skyline. Thankfully their passing is likely to be brief, after which the grey curtain once again descends.

Cam End, marked by a signpost, is the highest point on our walk. From here, bear right down an obvious track to join, albeit for a short spell, the celebrated Pennine Way. Accompany this clear trail between low grassy hillocks into the.constricted valley of Ling Gill. On reaching the stone footbridge spanning the beck, leave the Pennine Way, continuing on this side of the watercourse and swinging right to follow a wall up to New House Barn.

Immediately beyond the barn, close to some sheep pens, mount a stile on the left. Now heading south-west with the wall on your left and a fence high on the right, follow this elongated field, slanting away from the wall at its top end to cross a fence stile. Below left, the tree-lined vale of Ling Gill meanders onward to merge with the infant Ribble near Selside.

With the fence now on your right, stick with it up to a walled corner. Mount the stile to continue alongside the wall over a fence stile and across a depression. Surge up the far side, roller-coasting down to the isolated farming settlement of Nether Lodge. This lone farm is soon left behind as we swing sharply to the right, heading north-west to fork away from the access track. The reedy path skirts the base of Swinesett Hill before mounting the grass bank opposite and aiming towards a fence dividing the grassy ocean of Ling Gill Rigg. After this, lean half left into a marshy depression and up the far side of this roller-coaster terrain to gain a wall stile on Tile Hill. Stick with the wall on your left for 100 metres until the faint path forks away above a collapsed limekiln.

It then bears right up to a large barn. Mount the wall stile circling right behind the barn to climb Back Hools Hill beside a wall. Pass through a gap on the crest to drop down the far side to reach Thorns. A ladder stile adjoining this abandoned farmstead and a small gate will bring you into a rough, walled lane.

Spirits of the long departed hover around this hauntingly silent place, the bones of a once thriving settlement draped in bright green moss. Open to the elements, this unyielding landscape has now reclaimed its own. Nothing epitomises the finite quality of life quite so vividly than to stand in silent communion amidst the decaying remnants of a community long since forgotten.

Pause awhile to capture the ambience of this special locale before strolling up to the end of the corridor, where a ladder stile gives access to the open fell. Follow the wall on your left, sticking close when it veers away left over a rise then down into the vale occupied by Gayle Beck. Pay close attention to the striated bed of the stream where criss-crossed channels have been worn in the limestone.

Then cross the beck by means of the footbridge, leaning half right to mount a wall stile in front. Climb out of the valley and walk across a field to enter the back garden of Gearstones Lodge by a fence stile, followed by a gate to gain the main road. The original highway passed immediately in front of the old inn, which is below the present road.

This walk provides the opportunity to sample a lesser-known aspect of the Dales topography, far removed from the glossy postcard image of more favoured locations. Bleak windswept moorland does, however, personify vast areas of this most captivating of National Parks.

15. Cowan Bridge

Elementary Detection

Mystery: Masongill House, GR 666754

Distance Walked: 5 miles

Total Height Climbed: 400 feet, 122 metres

Start/Finish: Turn off the north side of the A65 along a side lane signposted to Masongill. Plenty of parking space is available at the top end of the village, near to the telephone box.

Terrain: Undulating, gently graded foothills comprising small enclosed fields with indistinct footpaths.

Nearest Shops: Cowan Bridge

Map Required: Ordnance Survey 1:25000 Outdoor Leisure 2, Yorkshire Dales Southern & Western areas

Drive along the A65 between Kirkby Lonsdale and Ingleton on any weekend of the year to witness the constant buzz of motorcyclists 'burning rubber'. When added to the flow of regular traffic using this important thoroughfare from West Yorkshire to the Lake District and all stops between, this is, indeed, one busy stretch of tarmac. Yet how many of these travellers bother to cast more than a cursory glance to right or left? Very few I would suggest, except perhaps to marvel at the geometric sculpting of Ingleborough's uniquely carved profile.

In consequence they remain ignorant of the literary associations known only to the discerning minority. The Brontë connection at Cowan Bridge has already been referred to in Mysterious Walks in Lancashire, and now just inside the Yorkshire Dales boundary the Doyle affinity is revealed. For tucked away up the cul-de-sac that peters out on the fell above Masongill lived Mary Doyle, a Scottish lass who gave birth to the eminent creator of Mr Sherlock Holmes.

Although many of the great sleuth's adventures occurred in and around London, his patron spent much time at Masongill walking on the fells. Moorstone Crag overlooking Kingsdale was one his favourite haunts where he spent many hours revelling in the glorious views. Whether the author was the illegitimate offspring of Masongill House's autocratic owner has never been revealed, the documents having been destroyed soon after Brian Waller's demise in 1932. Certainly Dr. Waller made it his business to

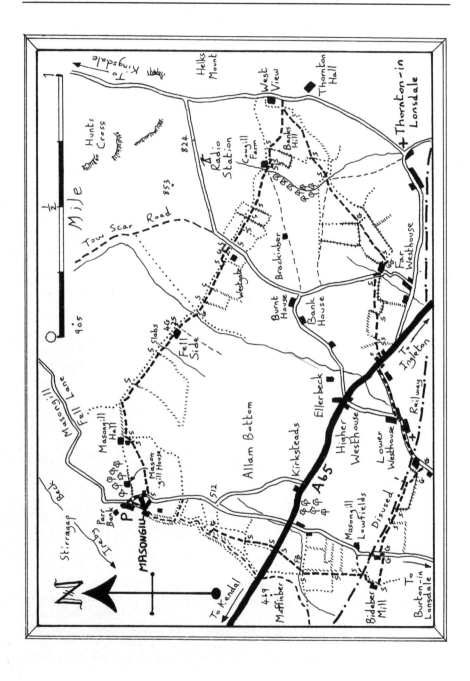

assist the young Doyle in his studies, although the latter made no secret of his unease regarding the doctor's relationship with his mother.

His widow, who clearly felt aggrieved at her husband's frequent liaisons with their attractive neighbour, erased all reference to the man's shady dealings with Mary Doyle. We can only surmise as to what life must have been like for a woman whose husband flitted between the family home at Masongill House and the small cottage across the fields.

Dr Waller met Mrs Doyle whilst lecturing at Edinburgh University, the young impressionable woman being drawn to the gallant doctor when her alcoholic artist husband was confined to a mental institution. Both parties had literary backgrounds, which is a strong indication of how the young Conan Doyle chose this avenue to make his singular mark upon the world. It also seems that Holmes the detective acquired his forename from two local clergymen based at Bentham.

Doyle married Louisa Hawkins in 1885 at Thornton-in-Lonsdale church and two years later the legendary investigator made his debut in A Study in Scarlet. Even after he achieved national acclaim, the author never forgot his roots, paying frequent visits to Masongill and writing over 1500 letters to his mother throughout their time apart.

Following Brian Waller's death, his widow shut herself away and lived a frugal life, keeping the house shuttered to discourage visitors. Amble back up the access road serving Masongill to a cottage on the left. Could this be where the young Conan Doyle spent his early years? Immediately beyond, go through a stile and across the large field with Masongill House, ensconced within an arboreal scarf, commanding the eastern prospect.

Aim for the far left corner close to the outer buildings of Masongill Hall, clearly a working farm unlike its purely residential neighbour. Cross the farm road to mount a ladder stile and accompany the hedge on your left up a gentle slope to the top end of the field. Bear right along the wall, over two stiles and a slabbed footbridge to reach Fell Side.

Keeping left of the farm buildings, pass through four gates and over two stiles to gain the fields at the far side. Stick with the continuing wall down into a deep cutting to straddle the slender ribbon of the beck. Open a gate to climb the opposite bank, mounting two stiles on the approach to Westgate. Bestride a stile at the wall corner to continue on the far side up to a fenced enclosure where a gate and stile will deposit you on Westgate Lane, an access highway for the valley of Kingsdale.

Cross straight over another stile on the far side to stroll along the right side of a wall. Ignore any disruption to the lie of the land caused by a new water main that has been installed between Westgate and Thornton-in-Lonsdale (summer 1999). It might well have reverted to natural pasture when you pass this way, which is an aim usually achieved successfully by the public utility companies.

From Westgate Lane count off four stiles, which will bring you to a large sloping field. Carry on to pass through the abandoned farmstead of Cowgill, stiled at each end. Another 50 metres and over the next stile, slant half right down another large sloping pasture towards West View. On reaching the walled limits round the house, cut back sharp right along the lower edge of Bank Hill. After 200 metres, veer away from the hedge boundary along an obvious grass shelf to locate a wall stile.

Then drop down to the opposite corner of the next field. Once over this stile cross a narrow Cow Gill, following the wall on your left until it slants away to the right. At this point the excavated water main is crossed – it is stiled at each side. Keep ahead thereafter on a direct course aiming for a gate at the far side of the field. Then stay parallel with the wall/hedge on the right to reach the hamlet of Far Westhouse.

Mount the wall stile, continuing ahead to then lean right to pass through a private garden, the owner of which acknowledges the right of way for walkers. This will deposit you on a back lane where a right for 100 metres will bring you to a stile on the left just beyond a small road bridge. Follow the fence up a rising slope, maintaining a straight course when this veers away left. Cross the open section of field to a stile at the far side in a hedge.

Two stiled barriers follow another open stretch and then it is downhill to the main road, gained between two houses. When I descended this last field in summer it was the sole preserve of rampant bulls that paid no heed to this obvious right of way, regarding me as a trespasser in their domain. Huffing and snorting with indignation, this was clearly not the time to argue the finer points of the Country Code. A rapid exit was called for to avoid the impending confrontation. You have been warned!

Bear right towards Kirkby Lonsdale for 100 metres then its left down a side lane through Lower Westhouse. Largest of the Westhouse collection, boasting a chapel and village hall, it is nevertheless passed through in the flicker of a gnat's wing. After sliding 'under' what used to be a bridge carrying the dismantled railway line over the road, enter the yard of Westhouse Lodge by a gate. Exit through a small gate to reach the field behind. Join with a field track but when it crosses the old railway, continue alongside the adjoining fence to parallel the cutting all the way to a back lane reached through a gate. Cross straight over through another gate to pass behind a large bungalow and over this field to arrive at Bideber Mill.

A stile followed by a few steps brings you to the yard of this old corn mill now converted to a dwelling house. Head right along the service track that takes you under the railway bridge to locate a stile on the left. Strike up the hill in front, heading due north soon alongside a hedge. Mount a stile to crest the hill, bowling down the far side to a wall where a gap remains hidden until the last minute. Lean half right over a small footbridge and over the field to reach and cross the main road.

A youthful Conan Doyle often visited this house at Masongill

On the far side, climb up the banking and over a stile to follow a wall on your left down to the corner where a stepped stile is crossed. Then walk over to the hedged-in track and follow its right-hand edge up to the top of the field, where a gate allows access to the track. Head right along this meandering old highway and imagine how all routes in rural communities must have been like this in the days of our ancestors. On arrival at a T-junction, take the track heading left into the outer reaches of Masongill. Slant right along a paved lane, back to its merger with the fell road.

A pleasant, easy-going ramble across the low foothills of this southern boundary of the Yorkshire Dales, this route is likely to remain outside the normal walking itinerary and should be conducted at a leisurely and sedate pace. The only encounters with other beings are likely to be glimpses of a spectral Conan Doyle roaming his beloved fells, perhaps accompanied by a retinue of fairies he claimed were resident on Thornton Fell.

16. Ingleborough
Mountain Fortress

Mystery: An Iron Age Settlement, GR 741745
Distance Walked: 6½ miles
Total Height Climbed: 1550 feet, 473 metres
Nearest Shops: Ingleton
Start/Finish: Two miles south-east of Ingleton along the old road to Clapham there is a pull-in adjacent to the High Leys access track at GR 719715.
Terrain: Rough walking for much of the way making use of clear tracks on limestone.
Map Required: Ordnance Survey 1:25000 Outdoor Leisure 2, Yorkshire Dales Southern & Western areas

Ingleton basks in the shadow of its namesake, the mighty Ingleborough

Although it cannot claim to be the highest of the mountains in the Yorkshire Dales, Ingleborough certainly enjoys the most popularity. And rightly so! Its knotty, isolated profile is compelling from all directions, acting as a magnet for those who love and revere the fell country of Northern England. Like the jutting prow of an ancient galley, it cleaves the ozone, scattering all pretenders to its lofty throne into disarray.

This particular ascent may not be the most exciting, nor even the most challenging route up the mountain but the walk does, in my view, qualify as the least known and you are unlikely to meet any other people until the summit plateau is reached. Undoubtedly it is the easiest ascent from valley level of any mountain exceeding the magical 2000ft contour in the country, the summit being gained with barely a slackening of pace. Unless, of course, you know different.

As far as Little Ingleborough the route accompanies a shepherds' track crossing a bleak wilderness where craters known as shake holes pockmark the arena like a First World War battlefield. These sinkholes are the result of dissolving limestone and frequently grow into full-blown potholes allowing entry to the subterranean White Scar cave system below. At one time it was thought that holes such as Gaping Gill were the source of the great flood waters that Noah managed to survive.

The area that encompasses Ingleborough is indeed riddled with tunnels and linked galleries, and it was these caves that first initiated the interest of the first tourists in the 18th century. Thomas Gray visiting the Ingleton Falls in 1769 commented that the village lay "at the foot of that huge monster of nature – Ingleborough". Over the following century, the celebrated walk around the falls attracted thousands of devotees, assisted in their quest by the provision of frequent railway specials.

Realising that the north of England offered more than just sheep and moorland, the more adventurous were encouraged to accompany local guides into the deep chambers. One such leader was a certain William Wilson who was "furnished with the necessary apparatus of a lanthorn, long candlestick, etc for the purpose" and entertained his clients with lurid adventures of his soldiering days.

From the roadside pull-in, a rough track leaning right should be followed round to a wall stile close to some sheep pens. Join the track heading up the grassy slopes of Cock Flower Hill parallel to the intake wall. A thin path soon forking right can be taken if you wish to cross the limestone outcropping of Grey Scars. Return to the main path higher up, north of the prominent cairn.

Our way keeps left of the Scars. When it slants sharply to the right, the jutting profile of Ingleborough hoves into view. Continue up the path towards the blunted shoulder of Little Ingleborough, passing close to a sheepfold. The prominent cairn on the horizon lies below the ridge top and adjacent to a rake, after which the main path from Clapham is joined. After the first limestone collar the route levels out, eventually climbing up the stony eastern rampart that encircles the citadel above. Bear left onto the summit plateau and head due west past a series of large cairns to the principal heap near to the crosswall shelter.

This was constructed to celebrate Queen Victoria's diamond jubilee and offers vital protection from the rampant westerlies. One observer of the

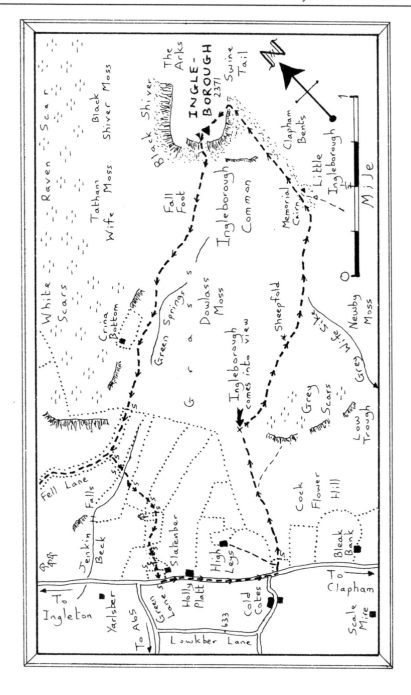

time reckoned that there were sixty fires lit on the summit that particular night, the glow being evident from far-off Bradford.

Adopted as a Brigantean stronghold during the Iron Age, Ingleborough survived intact for centuries until its final stand against the Romans in AD74. Ancient hut circles can be picked out around the disintegrating ramparts that once protected the inhabitants. It is doubtful if the fort was ever in permanent residence due to the excessively severe winters that would have been experienced at such an altitude. Nevertheless, it can claim the distinction of being the highest defensive site in England.

In 1830 a Mr Hornby Roughsedge, whose main residence was at Hornby Castle down the Lune valley, owned the Manor of Ingleborough. To commemorate the acquisition of this vast tract of land, he built a turreted hospice on the summit of the mountain. Following the consumption of an excessive amount of the celebratory beverage provided by the landlord, some of the workmen proceeded to pull the tower down. Roughsedge was so incensed by this wanton act of pre-Victorian vandalism that he stormed off back to Ingleton vowing never to return, a pledge that was stoically upheld.

A steep descent of the millstone grit cap heads south-west and pursues a direct course across the acres of peat mossland down to the isolated farmstead of Crina Bottom. Beyond here, maintain a level course to the right of a dry valley on the approach to the intake wall. Mount a stile into a walled corridor known as Fell Lane. Then look out for a stile on the left after a quarter mile.

Over this, follow the wall on your right, mounting another stile to drop down into the cutting occupied by Jenkin Beck. Climb out over a broken wall soon followed by solid wall stile. Head south-west crossing two more wall stiles, after which an unusual twin-trunked tree is passed on the right.

Cross a stile at the bottom of this field and stroll alongside a wall to another at the far end. Stick with this wall, now on the right and then on the left, until the last small enclosure is crossed to reach the Old Road. Bear left past the farm buildings of Slatenber for a stroll of less than a mile back to the start.

17. Austwick
The Wisdom of Simplicity

Mysteries: Austwick Creelies, GR 7668; Norber Erratics, GR 766699
Distance Walked: 7 miles
Total Height Climbed: 850 feet, 260 metres
Start/Finish: Sufficient parking space is available on the main street in Austwick near to the Game Cock Inn.
Terrain: Grass pastures surrender to eroded limestone pavements above Norber, where paths are indistinct.
Nearest Shops: Austwick
Map Required: Ordnance Survey 1:25000 Yorkshire Dales Western area

A secret gem removed from the bustling highway that skirts the western edge of the Yorkshire Dales National park, Austwick remains a backwater that most travellers only see on a signpost. Those who deviate from the main artery are invariably taking a short cut across the Wharfe Gap to Ribblesdale. Laid back in the manner of an action-replay, this easy-going community harks back to a past that has dissolved in the nebulous mists of time.

Even the old signpost beside the market cross is of a prime vintage and includes a grid reference for those who have gone astray. Of primordial heritage, behind the village the elongated grass terraces known as 'lynchets' are still visible where the sloping terrain was ploughed up, corn being the principal crop.

Being such a sleepy hollow and used to conducting its affairs within the confines of the village, locals were less than keen on outsiders attempting to change their cherished way of life. So when events took a decidedly laborious turn, villagers suddenly began to engage in peculiar behaviour intended to give the impression they were 'up the pole', 'round the twist', 'two pints short of a gallon'. Take your pick! They all meant the same thing, that locals were simpletons, or carles in the local parlance.

One occurrence concerned the cuckoo which brought fine weather in the spring until it emigrated in the autumn. In order to retain the bird throughout the year, the men held hands in a circle around the tree where the bird was nesting with the intention of caging it in. As a result of this story spreading across Yorkshire, the village became known as Cuckoo Town.

The market cross and vintage signpost in Austwick

Another farmer needed to move a bull from his field and called for eight volunteers to help lift it over the gate. One man needed to deliver a wheelbarrow to the next village but instead of taking the usual route along the road decided to go across country. By choosing this short cut he had to lift the heavy implement over twenty-five stiles.

The most recent event tells of the village brass band involved in a competition at Bradford, which they actually won. Not the sort of performance one would normally expect from carles. But on their return to Austwick following a celebration, the conductor told the players to keep quiet so as not to disturb the rest of the village. Obligingly, they removed their boots and marched down the main street in socks – playing a victory anthem at full blast.

Maybe in the past Austwick people did earn themselves a reputation for simplemindedness, but remember that it was a deliberate ploy to preserve a way of life they held dear. So who are we to blame them. Today, nobody who chooses to live in such a delightfully quaint locale could ever be labelled a carle.

Amble down the village street, forking left up a lane immediately beyond the primary school. On reaching the last house, lean right through its garden (gated at either side) to then enter a field by a stile. Accompany a grooved rake beside the wall on your right up to the ancient highway known as Thwaite Lane, which links Clapham with the hamlet of Wharfe. Cross straight over this walled track, stiled at each side, and follow the wall down to the end of the next field.

Mount a stile followed by a plank footbridge spanning Norber Sike to ascend the facing slope to a ladder stile at the top end. Here Crummack Lane is crossed and a wall followed up to the dark striated crag of Nappa Scar. Pass along the lower edge of the gritstone crag to straddle a wall just beyond. Lean half left over to the next wall stile, after which a thin trod meanders between a scattered array of chunky limestone boulders. Look out for a clear path slanting across the low scar ahead. Above lies the broad shelf of Norber and here is to be found a mystery of solid proportions. How have the huge layered rocks come to rest on small plinths of pale limestone, giving the appearance of giant mushrooms?

Known as 'erratics', they were deposited by a glacier when it melted at the end of the last Ice Age. Their origins are located higher up the valley and they are a unique feature of the karst landscape that characterises the Craven Dales. Before the solution to the enigma was revealed by the science of geology, strange mystical connotations were attached to the boulders and it was thought the hand of some primeval leviathan had placed them there.

The key role that ice has played in the shaping of the landscape never ceases to fascinate and is the principal reason why such areas have become so popular. Consideration of the ease with which these mammoth boulders were moved so easily from their source is nature's way of warning us not to take the land for granted. Respect and appreciation go hand in glove, such that we must always protect our natural heritage and help preserve it for future generations to enjoy.

A thin trail picks a delicate course through the chaotic splay of rocks, aiming for the wall corner above and to the right. Mount the ladder stile, taking a wide left-hand loop to make a gradual ascent onto the main plateau. Pathless, our route takes advantage of a shallow depression devoid of loose detritus as the wall running the length of the ridge is approached.

Before reaching the wall, swing right across the highest part of the broad ridge, following a series of widely spaced cairns. The light grey expanse of eroded limestone pavement gives the impression of a lunar landscape, barren and wild yet hauntingly beautiful. But if mist should envelop this stark wilderness, lean to the west and follow the wall down to the first stile encountered.

Otherwise, stay with the crest until the limestone cloak surrenders to a more grassy aspect. On the approach to a prominent cairn on rising ground, fork away left down towards a wall corner where a clear track is joined. Linking Clapdale and Crummack, accompany it down over a wall stile to

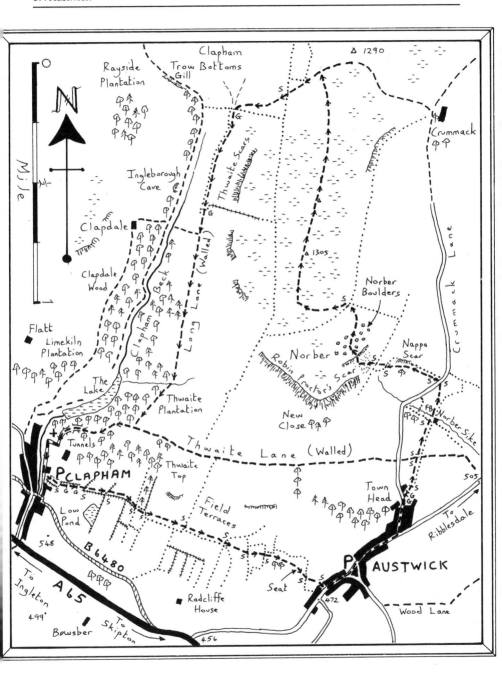

meet the start of Long Lane. Initially walled on the valley side only, this clear fell track heads due south for a little over 1½ miles down this side of the valley. Watch for the entrance to the main cave on the far side of Clapdale, this being the tourist entrance to the subterranean network of tunnels beneath the Ingleborough Massif.

Above it is Clapdale Hall, which was home to a certain Dame Alice who became known as the 'Clapham Witch'. Alice was foster mother to a young lad who lived at the hall whom she worshipped with more than just her soul. So fond was she in fact, that she made a pact with the Devil himself to ensure the boy's success in life. This agreement involved a list of tasks that were laid down and had to be performed to Old Nick's satisfaction, one of which included a visit to the bridge adjoining the parish church at midnight. There she was required to lay nine dead cocks in a circle and brush the water of the stream back up Clapdale. A somewhat difficult operation for Joe Public perhaps, but not to an experienced witch of Alice's reputation, who never failed in her endeavours.

With this in mind, continue down Long Lane to a T-junction, there heading right down into Clapham. Bear left down the main street of the village then left again at the National Park Information Centre. A narrow path squeezes between a hedge and fence along the edge of the car park, with a kissing gate at the end. Thereafter, head left along a right of way that follows the grass verge of a field access road through two swing gates until the fields proper are reached.

Keep heading east, initially through a stile with a fence on your right. This is the ancient pathway connecting Clapham with Austwick and is a joy to walk. Savour it at a relaxed pace, sticking to the fence through another stile up to the lower edge of Thwaite Top Plantation. A pair of stiles at either side will see you accompanying a wall on the right past an old gravel pit up to the next stile.

All field boundaries are drystone-walled from this point as we pass the terraced field system that our agrarian ancestors established long before the current network of fields was enclosed. Stay close to the wall on your right to the next stile, followed by two more in quick succession. Try to pick out the foundations of where the Neolithic settlement was situated.

Then pass along the top edge of a small copse before slanting down between another batch of lynchets to the next stile. Beyond this the path finds the only opening between the buildings on the outskirts of Austwick that gives on to the main street. Then bear left for 200 metres back to the centre of the village.

There is no reason to suppose that all who partake in this 'simply' marvellous circuit around the moonscape of Norber should not enjoy a superb walk of enduring impressions. It affords the opportunity to visit classic limestone terrain that harmonises with the subdued lowland pastures – in short, a bewitching experience.

18. Langcliffe
Forcing the Issue

Mysteries: The Winskill Bard, GR 827665; Robin's Mill, GR 818673
Distance Walked: 5 miles
Total Height Climbed: 600 feet, 183 metres
Start/Finish: After turning off the B6479 into Langliffe, which is located one mile north of Settle, drive through the village and use the car park adjacent to the primary school.
Terrain: Valley pastures give way to rough grazing on the exposed higher fell, all enclosed by drystone walls.
Nearest Shop: Langcliffe
Map Required: Ordnance Survey 1:25000 Outdoor Leisure 2, Yorkshire Dales Southern & Western areas

Market cross and fountain at Langcliffe

'Gateway to the Yorkshire Dales' is a particularly apt logo for the town of Settle, situated as it is across the mouth of Upper Ribblesdale. The limits of the National Park's southern boundary are marked by the limestone scarring of the Craven district, breached at this point by the River Ribble which has carved an elongated trough in the bedrock deep into the heartland of the 'Three Peaks' country.

Driving north up the valley, the first village encountered just a mile from Settle is Langcliffe, whose rain-washed cottages have changed little over the centuries. Lorries and caravans have no place here, the road beyond up Langcliffe Brow being an impossible haul for such vehicles. The village green boasts an elegant cross in memory of those who died in the

Great War. Now turned into a fountain, non-drinkable water spews from the mouths of leaden gargoyles. Far more dominant, however, is the Big Tree, a sycamore encased in a fence and surrounded by benches.

Take the track between houses and school at the edge of the village, leaning right along a walled access route serving the northerly pastures. At the end of this corridor, pass through a gate and accompany the wall on your right up to another gate. Ahead, the precipitous cliffs of the old limestone quarry dominate the view.

Our path now begins to climb across the open fields of Dicks Ground, passing through a broken wall gap before striking up the steepening slope. Rising through the loose scattering of trees, the path avoids the abrupt rift of Stainforth Scar to reach a gate. The gradient eases above the treeline, going through a wide gap to reach a wall stile on the left.

Crossing the level grass field, pay attention to the farmhouse on the left set back from the scar's acclivitous downfall. This is Low Winskill and was the home of a certain Thomas Twistleton. Clearly a man of more than average intellect for the time, Tom was a thinker who set his thoughts down on paper at the end of a hard day's graft in the fields.

More than just an ordinary Victorian hill farmer, he feared the decline of local dialects in favour of a less expressive form of communication and did his best to preserve its usage through the medium of poetry. Rhyming apparently came naturally to the burly Dalesman and his odes covered the whole gamut of life encompassing the valley communities. His perseverance reaped dividends in 1867 when a collection of his work was published under the heading of Splinters struck off Winskill Rock. Whether or not it became a bestseller is not recorded, although it may well have enabled him to retire from farming at the remote house on Winskill for his later years were spent at Burley, over the fells in Wharfedale, where he died in 1917.

Join the walled access lane exclusive to Low Winskill by a stile, heading right to another stile at the end. We now meet the track serving the neighbouring farm of High Winskill, which is slightly removed away to the left. Crossing straight over, accompany the wall on your left across undulating rough grazing up to a stile. The wall funnel on the far side soon opens out as we descend to meet the fell track linking Stainforth with the fell road.

Make a right to pass through a gate, following the track down to a stile where it enters a walled corridor that will transport you unerringly down to Stainforth. But first, straddle the stile on the right and accompany a thin trail meandering down into the depths of Stainforth Beck. The necessity of having to retrace your steps back to the main track should in no way deter you from undertaking this imperative exploration.

At the bottom of the rift, shrouded by a dense curtain of trees, cast your

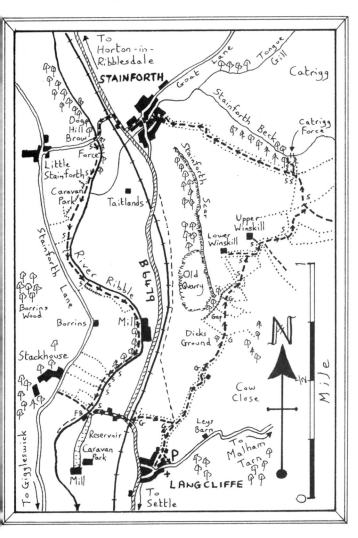

gaze upstream where a weakness in the underlying limestone strata has been exploited in dramatic fashion. Plunging over a notched lip, the double cascade makes an awe-inspiring sight that has to be one of the finest in the Dales. Yet Catrigg Force remains virtually unknown, lying off the beaten track – a feature that merely adds to its haunting allure.

Returning to the main track continue down into Stainforth, slanting left at the village green for 50 metres until a set of white posts is reached. Lean right here to gain the secluded bank of Stainforth Beck then left to reach the Craven Heffer Inn. A right will see you crossing the beck then a left takes you down to the main road. Turn right up the valley for 200 metres then head left down a narrow lane that swings down into the valley to cross the River Ribble by means of a splendid old packhorse bridge.

Dating back more than three centuries, the bridge links Knight or Little Stainforth with its more dominant neighbour and was commissioned by the monks of Sawley Abbey to replace the ford. Edward Elgar kept a photograph of the bridge in a prominent position and it features on the celebrated Elgar Way. Its elegant contours offer a beguiling tableau of stylish proportions from which to contemplate the swirling current beneath.

If you stand on the bridge and look upstream, the rocks on the left bank are all that remains of Robin Hood's Mill. Could this be the same character I revered in my youth? Perhaps, but in name only I suspect. It was rumoured that the avaricious owner of the mill kept it grinding out corn even on a Sunday to expand his wallet. His reward was to witness the mill disappearing down the cracks in the riverbed, where it continued to grumble and growl, just like the Devil's Mustard Mill at Kirkby Stephen in Cumbria.

A more prosaic explanation investigated in the 1930s by potholers suggests that the spluttering and gurgling is merely the result of subterranean watercourses echoing through the cave system hereabouts. Cock an ear in the direction of the old mill and listen hard. Surely that unearthly rumbling emanates from something more profound than water. I like to think so anyway.

Judge for yourself before heading downstream, following the right bank of the river and soon arriving at Stainforth Force that tumbles over a rock bar. Bubbling and foaming like brown ale, some say that the plunge pool is bottomless. Rich in salmon that are encouraged to swim upstream using 'ladders', the best time to witness the magical phenomenon of these lustrous creatures leaping up the falls is in late summer. Truly, this is a memorable sight and should not be missed.

However, should your luck be on its holidays, keep walking downstream along this section of the path that forms part of the Ribble Way. A half mile after passing the large factory on the opposite bank, you will reach a footbridge spanning the river just below a weir. It was this and others like it that made salmon ladders necessary if the fish were to reach their spawning grounds.

At the far side of the river, bear left up the lane to reach the main road. Take a right over the railway bridge then hard left along a short track for 50 metres only. Wander through the gate on the right, accompanying the wall on the left up to another gate giving onto the outward walled track. Head right to retrace your steps back into Langcliffe.

No ghosts should be encountered on this walk but some unusual sights sprinkled with local character second to none make for a walk to remember.

19. Giggleswick

Well Placed for a Laugh

Mysteries: Ebbing and Flowing Well, GR 804654; St Alkelda, GR 811641

Distance Walked: 5 miles

Total Height Climbed: 600 feet, 183 metres

Nearest Facilities: Giggleswick

Start/Finish: Approaching Settle from the north along the old road now renamed the B6480, fork right along the lane just beyond the golf course. Park on the open verge on the right after a quarter of a mile.

Terrain: Scenery characteristic of the limestone dales with abruptly exposed scarring and grass pastures enclosed by grey stone walls.

Map Required: Ordnance Survey 1:25000 Yorkshire Dales Western area

Giggleswick: renowned for its school and a watery legend

Although somewhat overshadowed by a renowned public school, Giggleswick has much to smile about having lost none of its graceful charm. Now that traffic has been diverted onto the bypass that avoids Settle altogether, the village has been effectively consigned to a rural backwater. A peace and tranquillity not enjoyed for generations has now descended on this ancient seat of learning.

To reach the village, continue down the lane past various annexes belonging to the school and watch for a narrow wall gap on the left. Go down a flight of stone steps, take the footpath beside the playing fields and eventually arrive at the 'towering' church of St Alkelda by means of two slim gap stiles. A brown, wooden gate allows entry to the churchyard where Giggleswick's most colourful resident lies buried.

Before his death from liver disease in 1988, Russell Harty ensured that Giggleswick became a household name. Arriving as a teacher at the prestigious school, he left as a television presenter of inestimable charisma. Broadcasting will never see his like again. Alan Bennett, the playwright, joked that Russell had nicked the cemetery plot that he had always coveted.

St Alkelda is thought to have been a lady of Saxon origin who baptised the faithful in the pure water from the numerous wells in the vicinity. A nebulous figure, it is said that two visiting Danes strangled her to death, a legend that is commemorated in the church's stained glass windows. A more likely association is the claim that Alkelda, meaning holy well, was a mythical nymph who was changed into a spring. It is known that in ancient times wells were worshipped as essential features of the community, often having magical properties attached to them. The only other church dedicated to this saint is at Middleham in the eastern dales where the same association has arisen.

Head west along the main street, past the market cross to the next left turning. On the corner is Cravendale, home to a certain Dr Charles Buck who befriended one of the finest musicians of his day. A talented conductor at the time, Edward Elgar often accompanied the doctor on walks around the district, which doubtless inspired his compositions. The Elgar Way is a tribute to the great man, linking places the pair often visited.

Return to the market cross. This epitomises a friendly if longstanding rivalry between Giggleswick and Settle which usually surfaces on the playing fields. This dispute began 200 years ago when Settle dignitaries claimed their opposite number across the River Ribble had stolen the revered cross as a challenge to Settle's market charter. The cross was never returned and here in Giggleswick it remains, in contrast to a fountain erected in 1863 on its original site in Settle.

Turn right up a narrow lane passing behind the Black Bull, where a hidden path begins in the far corner of the yard. Unseen until the last minute,

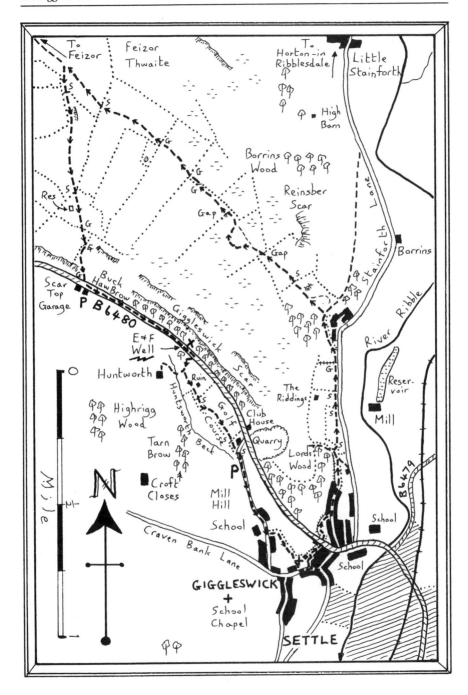

this walled passage offers an easy way up to the main road. Turn left at the top and go down for 20 metres, only crossing to ascend a flight of steps on the far side. Accompany a pinched corridor that goes between the houses, emerging on to an avenue of fine detached villas. Bear left to the end of the paved section, after which a rough track continues.

Keep with the track past a link forking in from the right until it bends left uphill adjacent to Lord's Wood. Then drop down a short yet steep incline to a ladder stile, so entering a walled corridor. Bear half right to a stile in the opposite wall and amble across the field to the far right corner and another stile close to Stainforth Lane.

Keep parallel to the lane crossing the access road serving The Riddings and on to the next stile. Still walking alongside the lane, you will eventually reach a gate at the far end of this field. Here our route leans away from the road, climbing gradually beside a wall above the village of Stackhouse. On reaching a signpost, head left uphill on a pathless tract in the direction of Feizor.

Maintain a straight course heading north-west up these low pastures, keeping left of a prominent outcrop to locate a ladder stile over the wall. Beyond here, head straight across to the far side of the field, aiming for the left of two large gaps in the wall ahead. Follow a clear field track that meanders up the rolling terrain comprising broken ribs of limestone.

On reaching a wall corner, continue along to pass through a gap, accompanying the wall on your right almost to the end of the field. Go through a gate and along the far side to another. With rising scars of silvery limestone controlling the right flank, cross open ground still on a straight course, passing through the next gate after 300 metres.

With a wall now on the left, the track crests the broad plateau leaning half left towards a stile in the wall ahead. The scabrous outburst of Smearsett Scar dominates the foreground above Feizor hamlet nestling in its own idyllic Utopia 'far from the madding crowd'. In the distance Ingleborough loses much of its dramatic appeal when viewed from this position.

Dropping down towards Feizor, watch for a signpost pointing the way due south to Buck Haw Brow. Swing sharp left here, keeping left of a wall to mount a ladder stile. Sandwiched between a low scar and the wall for 200 metres, the path then opens out across a sprawling grass patch keeping to a southerly tack. Beyond a wall stile at the far side keep left of a small walled reservoir, after which two walled gates are negotiated.

A sharp descent through a breach in the elongated reach of Giggleswick Scar will bring you down to Buck Haw Brow and Scar Top Garage. Now relegated to a B-road since the opening of the Settle bypass, the walk down towards Giggleswick is a far more pleasant experience than previously.

Relatively traffic free, the stroll down to the Ebbing and Flowing Well beneath the Scar is to be savoured.

Easily recognised on the left of the road, ensconced within a scarf of trees, the well is surrounded by stone benches. Rising and falling at decidedly irregular intervals, it is thought to be the result of a natural siphoning process within the rocks interacting with the pressures occasioned by subterranean watercourses. I hung around for the grand total of ten minutes without any change occurring, although a friend claims to have witnessed two alterations in a half-hour period. How lucky were you?

A more intriguing story relates to the 'satyr' whose lustful appetite for young maidens led to a spirited chase of one particular maiden that ended beneath Giggleswick Scar. Praying to the gods for help, she was turned into a well that immediately 'sprang' up, pulsating with the purest water. Thereafter the site became a sacred place for the baptising of converts to the Christian faith by St Alkelda.

Just beyond the well, take the track on the right, cutting back to cross the valley towards Huntworth. Before reaching the beck, slant left across a rough grassy knoll towards a wall corner opposite an old ruin beneath a crag. Accompany the left side of the wall up to a stile to enter the local golf course. Keep to the wall for a short distance before veering away left to reach the public footpath that cuts through the fairways.

Unfortunately, paracetamols are unlikely to cure the heaadache caused by contact with low flying golf balls so keep a look out. Ignore a clear track wheeling right into the adjacent field, which is now an extension of the golf course. Instead, keep ahead alongside the wall towards Tarn Barn where a stile at either side of the rough will bring you to the Giggleswick lane. Bearing right for 200 metres will return you to the start.

20. Wigglesworth

Doggedly Determined

Mystery: The Black Hound, GR 800565

Distance Walked: 5½ miles

Total Height Climbed: 200 feet, 61 metres

Start/Finish: Park on the wide grass verge in Wigglesworth. It is on the left immediately before the Y-junction when approaching from Rathmell.

Terrain: Enclosed grass pastures in this mid-section of Ribblesdale rise gradually on the western side to eventually merge with the Bowland Fells. Paths are indistinct all the way, making this an interesting test in route selection.

Nearest Shop: Wigglesworth

Map Required: Ordnance Survey 1:25000 Outdoor Leisure 41, Forest of Bowland & Ribblesdale

Uniquely different from the other walks in this guide, it introduces territory largely unexplored by others of the species, which in effect guarantees a degree of seclusion other parts of the Ribble Valley can only dream about. Solitary walkers can relish a sense of isolation normally felt only in remote wilderness areas.

But such a Utopia is not without its price. Footpaths are virtually non-existent, gates often being locked thus needing a leg over, and some fence boundaries lack stiles. This was not, however, the case with the drystone walls built when all rights of way were in regular usage. A test of your route-finding skills, and my descriptive talents will hopefully produce an enjoyable ramble.

A tiny settlement and one of a handful on this side of the River Ribble, Wigglesworth has been effectively bypassed by the main A65 linking the heartland of industrial West Yorkshire with north-west England. Traffic constantly streams along this busy thoroughfare with barely a glance to the west where low hills rise gradually towards the Bowland Fells. All eyes are invariable focused on the more dramatic limestone terrain that characterises the Dales National Park.

Barely more than a hamlet, Wigglesworth remains a backwater comprising a handful of stone cottages clustered about the Y-junction. The dominant feature is the Plough Inn, an elongated mock-Tudor hostelry with a commodious car park. Surprisingly for such a small settlement, Wigglesworth also boasts a post office/general store and adjacent garage.

Both of these premises in the early part of the 20th century were owned and run by the Mansergh family whose influence stretched as far as Kirkby Lonsdale. Robert Mansergh ran the provender store (now the post office) and later bought the adjoining premises to operate a service station, and it is to his granddaughter Margaret Shaw that thanks must be expressed for the following information about this much-loved local character.

He was the first person in the area to own a motorcycle and frequently upset the residents of Settle by roaring full pelt through the normally quiet streets on his new-fangled velocipede. In the days when most people travelled at an infinitely more sedate pace by horse and cart, this red-haired rider must have appeared like a rampant Viking warrior resurrected from the dead. More relevant to the mystery investigated on this walk is the fact that Robert owned a small dog that he employed to catch rats. In the back room where grain and other edibles were stored, the long-tailed in-

Becks Brow, near Wigglesworth, where lurks a mysterious black dog

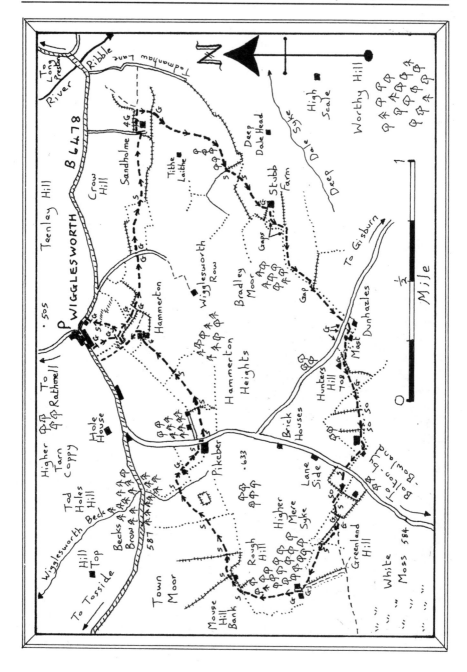

terlopers would creep in through numerous holes in the wooden floor. After blocking them off with scale weights, he placed the canny canine in front of the sole remaining hole to nab the unwelcome intruders as they emerged.

It was a successful ploy that netted many of the culprits but unfortunately went astray when one of the rats leapt over Robert's shoulder to escape the hound's terminating snappers. Lunging across to secure the crafty customer, the poor dog ripped a chunk from its hairy skin on a protruding nail. With its life in jeopardy, the local gamekeeper was quickly summoned to stitch up the wounded ratter – a task that was duly accomplished with aplomb. The offending grain grabber was lucky to escape with his own skin intact, until the next foray into the provender store.

Another one-off feature of this walk is that we do not actually visit the enigmatic site to which our mystery relates. The only existing right of way passes 200 metres behind the coniferous plantation of Becks Brow and is made use of towards the end of the walk.

So prior to setting out, drive straight through Wigglesworth, taking the road signposted to Tosside until it enters the gloomy stretch of conifers that flanks the road for a distance of a quarter mile. This is Becks Brow. And here it was that the Reverend John Robinson gave thanks for the presence of a mysterious black dog that had followed him all the way from Settle.

Secreted within the confines of the close-packed ranks of conifers, two felons set upon the unwary reverend with robbery clearly in mind. The dog immediately leapt on the callous duo and succeeded in frightening them off. It then continued to follow the vicar back to his chapel at Tosside. The next morning when the cleric went to feed his guardian angel, it had departed and was never seen again. Perhaps like the Good Samaritan of biblical repute, it had gone in search of another vulnerable traveller in need of protection.

On returning to Wigglesworth, stroll up the main street past the garage and take a left up a signposted track. A gate at the rear of the houses deposits you in a field that is crossed to its far side. Go through a small wooden gate in a wall and traverse the next field, funnelling into a corridor bounded by a wall and high wire fence. Mount a hurdle midway to pass through a gate at the end.

Entering a large irregular field, cross to its far side maintaining an easterly bearing. Once over a metalled back lane gated at either side, cross another field aiming towards the far right corner where a wall stile can be straddled. Lean away from the continuing fence on the right, making your way across to Sandholme. Keeping left of the house, count off four gates. This should see you entering a field at the other side.

With a fence on your left, amble up to the corner where a right of way crossroads is reached, although no visible signs can be seen on the ground to indicate the passage of feet. Bear right, heading south, to pass through a gate into a large open tract. Slant half right across to the upper limit of a line of trees then swing right to reach a fence.

Mount the stile then lean half left over to a wall stile, after which a brief rise will bring you to the gate giving access to Stubbs Farm adjacent to an old single-deck bus. Now utilised as a residence, I am reliably assured that it affords a cosy pad for winter hibernation. Head left along the farm track, which will take you all the way to the fell road opposite Dunhazles.

Go straight over through a gate, leaning right through another to avoid the farmyard. Cross to the third gate at the upper end of the field then stroll past the communications mast that provides the only significant landmark in the vicinity. After passing through the gate at the end, cut over to another in the fence.

Immediately in front is Hunters Hill, an important piece of raised real estate due to the Ordnance Survey having elected to build a trig column on its summit. In a locality where rocky outcrops are decidedly thin on the ground and where appendages such as 'pike' and 'crag' are completely absent, Hunters Hill assumes the status of an Ingleborough amidst the array of less influential 'hills'.

Having duly noted the prestige of this otherwise prosaic mound, head left alongside the wall down to a gate. Stick close to the wall, straddling two unstiled hurdles to reach Moss Side Farm (in a state of 'turbulent transition' when I passed this way in December 1999). Pick a route round to the front of the stone terrace before walking along the service track down to another fell road.

Opposite is a stile, then it's across to the far left corner to step over a hurdle minus the obligatory stile. Amble along the wall beyond up to a stepped stile then bear half left to pass through a fence gate. Make use of the next gate in a fence that reaches to the woodland in front and accompany this on its left side as far as the trees.

Mount a wall stile on the left but take special care with the electric fence that runs alongside. A warning is given and the landowner has seen fit to cover the exposed wire adjacent to the stile, which is to his credit. Keeping to the left side of the wood will bring you to High Mere Syke where a gate allows access to the farm track. Swing right through the yard, exiting by a gate at the far side. Cross the next field nudging the top corner of the woods and aiming for the right corner where a stile is mounted. Bear right over Mouse Hill Bank beside a fence straddling another stile immediately beyond a barn.

Bend right down to the next stile then maintain a north-westerly course, keeping watch for a gap stile in the wall ahead. Once over this, keep left round a fenced enclosure to drop down into the deep cutting occupied by Wigglesworth Beck. To your left rises the sinister swathe of dark conifers on Becks Brow where the Reverend Robinson was attacked. Let us trust that the elusive black dog frightened off the spirits of the roguish felons.

Step over the foaming brew to locate a stile in the wall that chaperones the far bank and climb up the slope, veering right towards Loscober Laith. Pass through the gate nearby then lean half left towards Pikeber. A stile on this side of the farm in the far corner gives onto the fell road. Head right for no more than 20 metres before mounting the stile on the opposite side of the road.

Traverse the field, keeping left of a strange circular copse surrounded by a wall to leap the fence stile, thereafter continuing onward to locate a wall stile adjacent to the field track. Stick to a straight course dropping gradually down to reach Hamerton. Go through the gate then bear left between the buildings for a stroll down the access track.

When the high wire fence swings right, accompany it through a gate and along a short link passage that opens out into the field where our outward trail is bisected. Keep ahead along the wall on the left to its corner, where a fence stile is straddled. Then it's down to the final gate adjoining a detached stone house. A stroll of 100 metres to the left will return you to the main junction opposite the Plough Inn at Wigglesworth.

21. Malham

Gorged on Limestone

Mysteries: Janet's Foss, GR 911633; Nevison's Leap, GR 916641
Distance Walked: 7 miles
Total Height Climbed: 650 feet, 198 metres
Start/Finish: A large official car park is located behind houses on the west side of Malham village. Alternatively, a start can be made from the fell road car park close to Malham Tarn.
Terrain: Classical limestone scenery of the highest quality with clear paths all the way.
Nearest Shops: Malham
Map Required: Ordnance Survey 1:25000 Outdoor Leisure 2, Yorkshire Dales Southern & Western areas

O f the various honeypots in the Yorkshire Dales, Malham offers the most exciting and dramatic landscape and can be viewed from a safe distance or experienced in the raw. This walk is a classic encompassing the entire gamut of textbook limestone terrain visited at close quarters. Nowhere else in Northern England exhibits such a spectacular gorge setting. Mind-boggling, awesome, grandiose – the epithets flick off the tongue in a never ending procession and no excuse is needed to continue. This is indeed a unique corner of England.

Formed at the end of the last Ice Age when melt water poured through fissures in the limestone bedding plains, the result was catastrophic. Such a landscape must have been designed by nature with fell trekkers in mind. Do not disappoint the architect.

So head south from Malham along the gravel track on the opposite side of the beck from the road, making use of a narrow footbridge spanning Malham Beck. Then bear right for 300 metres until a signpost points the way to Janet's Foss. After slipping through the stile, take a left up to a ladder stile just before Mires Barn, continuing up this side valley on the far side of the wall. Stroll on up to a double stile on either side of a walled field track.

The path forges ahead squeezed between the wall and Gordale Beck, passing right of New Laithe. Mount a stile soon after, the clear path bending left and negotiating two more stiles where it enters a wooded glen. On rounding a bend in this confined vale, the secluded grotto of Janet's Foss appears resplendent in its silvery cloak. Behind the enchanting cascade lies a small cave where Janet the 'Queen of the Fairies' is reputed to live.

On a trip through this part of the Dales in 1792, the future Viscount Torrington was so enamoured by the charming picture that he penned an ode called 'The Fairy's Dance', the first verse of which reads,

'Little Gennet, Fairy trim
To the merry dance leads on
Full of pastime, full of whim,
With her playmate, Oberon!'

More down to earth was the pool's use for sheep-washing. Unlike today when the fleece has become a liability to many hill farmers, it fetched a higher price after a thorough dousing. The dipping became a social occasion, which doubtless included a barrel or three of the resident brew carted up from the Lister Arms in Malham.

Climb left up the passage that soon brings you to the road where a right will find you crossing Gordale Beck by either the old or new bridge. Continue along the road, which now becomes Hawthorns Lane after a sharp swing to the right. Leave it immediately through a gate on the left, striding out across a level grass plain. Ahead, soaring tiers of limestone offer a tantalising taster of what is to come.

On reaching a wall the path keeps to the right as the valley sides close in, squeezing Gordale Beck out of the gorge like toothpaste. Upon swinging right into the deeply enclosed amphitheatre, hanging jaws are guaranteed as all who witness this startling fissure stand open-mouthed and awestruck, silenced by the fiercesome sight that assails the senses. Sheer cliffs loom up on all sides with the falls at the back of the ravine riven in two by thick deposits of calcium carbonate known as tuff.

Numerous giants of the literary world from the 18th century came to gaze upon this amazing spectacle, including William Wordsworth and Thomas Gray. The latter in 1769 asserted that the surging upthrust of naked rock "forms the principal horror of this place". As always, Wordsworth chose verse to elucidate his own thoughts, referring to:

'Gordale chasm, terrific as the lair
Where the young lions crouch'

For many who come to visit Gordale Scar, this is the end of the track. Ascent of the falls is a hazardous undertaking and not for the fainthearted, especially after rain when the limestone is greasy and very slippery underfoot. If your determination to continue overshadows any lingering doubts, cross to the left side of the gorge and beck.

My choice of ascent and that with most hand and footholds is the central buttress between the outpouring spouts. On reaching the upper level immediately above the falls, the towering walls are at their closest overhanging the closeted ravine. This is no place for those suffering from claustrophobia.

The gap has long been known as Nevison's Leap after the highwayman regarded by many countryfolk as the north's own Robin Hood. Robbing the rich to give the poor as the saying goes, Will Nevison led a charmed life and always managed to stay one step ahead of the law, and those who would betray him for the inevitable reward.

One old woman who had often benefited from Will's generosity lived in a cave near the Ebbing and Flowing Well below Giggleswick Scar (See Walk 19). Once while on the run, the exhausted fugitive was given a 'magic bit' made of silver by the old woman. She told him that it would confer supernatural powers on his jaded mount. Unable to rest for the night with the thief-takers in hot pursuit, Will spurred his mount onward. Aided by the magical talisman, the horse shrugged off its lethargy and flew over the crags until the pair finally arrived at Gordale Scar. With barely a hint of fatigue, man and beast leapt the mighty chasm. Nevison was astounded by such a mammoth jump – one that had never previously been achieved. With pursuit effectively stymied, the outlaw continued east to Percival Hall where he was again sure of a safe refuge (See Walk 29).

Like Jesse James across the big pond, Will Nevison before him was regarded with affection by many sections of the community that he helped. No ordinary footpad, King George, who is said to have chuckled heartily on hearing of the rascal's exploits, dubbed him "Swift Nicks". Peering up to the apex of this awesome rift, it may appear that only magical powers could have facilitated such a leap. That is the legend. I prefer to think that Will Nevison rode a horse of exceptional quality and stamina that pulled out all the stops at just the right moment.

A steep climb follows on the left side of the gorge, emerging onto the moor above as the ravine continues north to its climax. After mounting a stile, our route follows a wall on the right until the path forks away to the left close to a large white cairn. Heading north-west across the plateau between outcroppings of limestone pavement, the grass path veers towards a wall lining the fell road. Cross the stile adjacent to Seaty Hill on the right. This is an ancient burial mound where a skeleton was discovered, proving that there was indeed life here before Chris Tarrant.

Head north along the road, soon forking right on a track that sticks to the wall. On reaching a crossroads, go straight over along the continuing track that serves Middle House Farm – hidden from view on the far side of Great Close Hill. When this track passes through a gap in the cross wall, bear left alongside Great Close Plantation (in reality a tiny copse) and accompany the wall, keeping left of a fenced wood ahead, to gain the access road for Malham Tarn House.

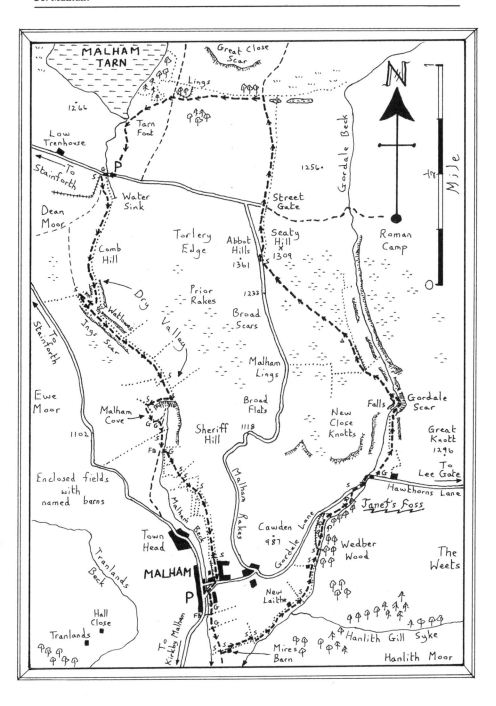

Aim left of the walled planting of conifers beyond the road, ambling down to the edge of Malham Tarn itself. The name is a misnomer as it still retains all the characteristics of a lake. Located on a plateau where the porous nature of the dominant limestone impedes what water courses exist, Malham Tarn is not only a permanent feature of the landscape but a substantial stretch that once extended over the mossland of Great Close. Impervious Silurian slate prevents the water filtering away, assisted by a glacial deposit of moraine damming the outlet flow.

Trout, which abound in the tarn, are thought to have been carried to this highest of the Dales lakes by the feet of birds. Nature conservation restricts public access to the shores apart from this nudge at the south-east corner. The house seen through the tree cover at the northern end, once the residence of a wealth industrialist called Walter Morrison, is now a field study centre.

Morrison bought the house in 1858 and made his pile from black crêpe used at funerals and investment in the Argentine railway network. Frugal in his lifestyle, the house reflected Morrison's abhorrence of ostentation. He enjoyed the simple country life far from urban influences and only later in life was persuaded first to rent then buy a motor vehicle.

In the days before the introduction of the driving test, Morrison was returning to the house with his recent purchase after only a cursory briefing. Turning into the yard he cried out, "Whooa lass! Whooa!" assuming the vehicle would stop of its own volition. This it certainly did by crashing into the gatepost. Driving for Walter Morrison was indeed a 'hit and miss' affair.

No such simple-mindedness is evident in his concern for education. In 1897 to celebrate Queen Victoria's Diamond Jubilee, he commissioned the chapel with its copper dome to be built at Giggleswick on a hill overlooking the school.

Veering away from the tarn, the path soon arrives at the fell road car park. Bear right along this through a gate and take the stile on the left, leaning half left towards a wall. On the far side of the wall, Malham Beck abruptly disappears into the bowels of the fell, squirming along the myriad of channels within the limestone beds to reappear down valley at the base of Malham Cove.

The intervening 1½ miles affords an impressive descent of the 'Dry Valley' sandwiched between layered scars of limestone. Choked with stones worn smooth by a regular procession of pilgrims who recognise the unique nature of the terrain, the path soon arrives at an acclivitous 80ft downfall. This was a splendid waterfall before the beck chose its subterranean course. Make a sharp detour right to cross the stile at the head of a tributary, descending a pinched groove to reach the valley floor.

With a wall on your left, stroll down to the end along flat bottomland devoid of any watercourse. After mounting a wall stile, continue onward for 100 metres until the broad limestone pavement above the Cove is reached. Clint blocks interspersed with worn channels known as grikes offer a sheltered environment allowing all types of plant life to flourish. Do not under any circumstances stray too near the lip of the overhang, unless, of course, you wish to test out a new parachute or practise bird impressions.

And in damp conditions when the pavement assumes the properties of a skating rink, keep to the rear where easier movement free from broken limbs and loss of dignity is possible. Cross to the western side of the pavement, dropping down to straddle a stile then veering left along a purpose-built stairway that winds down to the base of Malham Cove. Here the beck debouches from the gritty entrails of the mighty beast, which is here nought but a shallow gap. But for most people, it is the 240-foot vertical cliff racing skyward that transfixes the optics and stimulates the imagination. Unseen are the numerous fissures and underground passages that extend up to 600 metres from the entrance, culminating in a chamber referred to as Moon after a local farmer.

Drag yourself away from this wondrous dell to head downstream on a clear path. After passing through a stile, amble on for a further 100 metres until Moon Bridge is reached over Malham Beck on the left. Walk over this ancient clapper-style bridge composed of limestone slabs resting on pillars,

Moon Bridge offers an easy crossing of Malham Beck

which makes for a simple yet effective crossing that has ably resisted the ravages of time. Through the gate on the opposite side, slant right up a grassy slope to meet a wall on your right. Forge ahead to a stile at the far side of this walled meadow followed by another soon after. Descend an easy gradient funnelling into a passage containing a stile in its neck. Continue down across an open patch of greenery before lurching into a walled corridor that brings you down to the edge of Malham village.

Pass through a stile and down a side lane to reach the village centre with a youth hostel on the left. Lean right past the Lister Arms down to Monks Bridge, which was originally much narrower to accomodate packhorse traffic only. Keep this side of Malham Beck to rejoin the outward pathway. All that remains is to re-cross the footbridge to the main street.

And if anybody has not had their batteries recharged after this exciting and turbulent walk, I'll enter a monastery. The monks in these establishments often have spooky tales to tell!

22. Airton

A Grave Undertaking!

Mysteries: The Devil's Doing, GR 894610; A Watery End, GR 894610
Distance Walked: 8½ miles
Total Height Climbed: 650 feet, 198 metres
Start/Finish: Driving out of Hellifield towards Skipton on the A65, take the first lane forking left and signposted to Malham and Airton. After 2 miles, you will reach the village of Otterburn. Park on the wide verge on the left immediately beyond the track access known as Dacre Lane.
Terrain: Undulating grassy foothills divided into large pastures slope down to the Aire Valley.
Nearest Shops: Airton
Map Required: Ordnance Survey 1:25000 Outdoor Leisure 2, Yorkshire Dales Southern & Western areas

Green waves of rolling pastureland characterise the landscape on the southern boundary of the Yorkshire Dales National Park. Carved up by drystone walls, these low hillocks give the appearance of a green sea rising gradually to the north, where they surrender to the more abrupt limestone terrain most associated with the Dales.

Inherently sublime and attractively regal, this rural Utopia is covered by a multitude of farm tracks. However, you will be fortunate indeed to encounter others of the species en route – or unlucky depending on your viewpoint. My own preference leans towards a solitary enjoyment of the landscape. Yet this is not wildly unkempt moorland, far from it. In summer, rich grassland sways in syncopated harmony, with the gentle zephyrs blowing in from the west providing the essential hay crop for more inclement seasons.

Few motor roads traverse these airy foothills, further instilling a sense of isolation usually reserved for more lofty terrain. It is an experience to be savoured and relished, so head off up Dacre Lane which offers a direct route to Settle. Although a rough track, this was clearly in days past the main highway linking Otterburn with the principal town in the area.

After a mile, the Crook Beck Plantation is reached where a gate gives access to woodlands that encourage visitors to wander at will. But only in those owned by the Woodland Trust on the left. To the right there is a clear warning that these arboreal innards are private property, access being firmly denied. Perhaps at some stage in the not too distant future, these conflicting landlords can get together and resolve their differences to the benefit of us all.

At the far edge of the woods, exit via a gate to strike up the rising ground ahead, aiming for a gate on the near horizon and keeping to the right of a line of trees. Beyond is Hellifield Moor, the clear track surging across this open tract in a north-westerly direction. This is the only section of the walk where any resemblance to rough moorland is crossed. At the far side, pass through the left of two gates, continuing onward with a wall on the right. On reaching a stile the track is funnelled into a walled corridor. After 200 metres it drops down into a shallow depression where you should lean right to cross a wall stile. Follow the wall on your right over another until a merging of streams is reached.

Ford the infant Otterburn Beck to mount a wall stile forging up the grass bank in front and out of the valley. When the path fades, keep to a straight course, crossing a reedy hollow and going up the far side to mount a wall stile. Continue on the same course to the far side of the field and so arrive at the track serving Crake Moor, surely one of the most isolated farms in the vicinity. Go through the gate, heading right along the track to circle be-

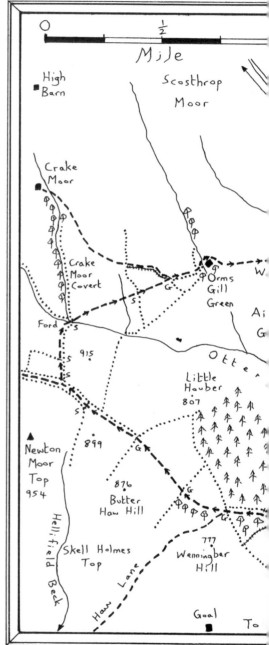

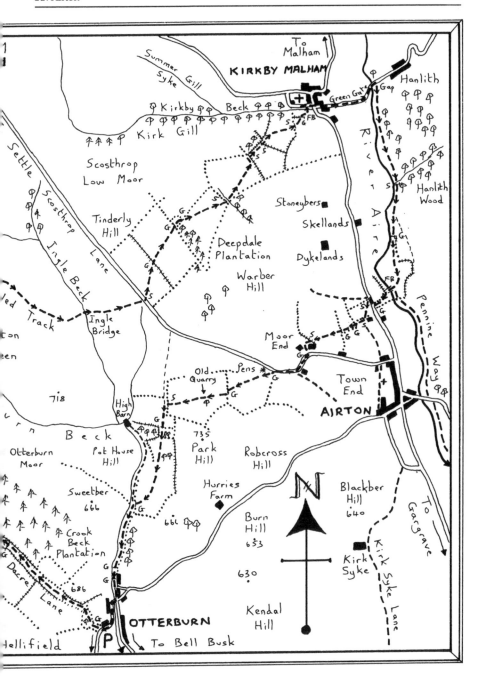

hind Orms Gill Green. Those of you hankering after the good life might well consider this locale to fit the bill admirably. Accompany this walled track all the way to Scosthrop Lane.

Slightly offset to the right is the continuation of our route. So mount the stile and follow it through a fence gate ahead and past an array of old quarry workings, aiming to the left of the trees ahead. Through the gate, hang right to another and so into the adjoining field. Steer a passage half left to the far corner, there to straddle a wall stile and dropping down to step over a narrow rill.

Beyond the line of trees, lean away to the left aiming towards the fence on the far side of the field, bearing left to the edge of a plantation. Mount the stile and head down a steepening gradient beside the fence. Cross the fence stile below, leaning to the right over to a wall stile further down.

Another 100 metres will see you opening a gate to enter the dense canopy of trees chaperoning Kirkby Beck. Descend a flight of cobbled steps into the sepulchral gloom to cross the beck by a footbridge. Emerging on a back lane, the church of St Michael the Archangel assaults the senses with its majesty and grace.

Removed from the normal tourist itinerary and of a size far exceeding the needs of the local populace, it remains aloof from the constant bustle of Malham itself to the north. Boasting an ancient lineage harking back to monastic connections, the church is well worth more than a cursory investigation. Of special interest to seekers after curious and eccentric phenomena is the Devil's Door that faces you on entering the church by the main porch. Now blocked off, this northern entrance was at one time always left open when christenings were being conducted for the sole purpose of enabling any evil spirits to escape.

Take a closer look at the old doorway and you will see a copy document inscribed with the signature of Oliver Cromwell. In 1655, the Lord Protector of England came to the Aire Valley and stayed at Calton Hall near Airton as a guest of General Lambert. Whilst there he witnessed a wedding between two local people, the ceremony being conducted at Middle House close to Malham Tarn (See Walk 21).

Back in the graveyard, any flat gravestone should be viewed with a modicum of caution – especially by those partial to a good nosh-up. Once again Old Nick's skulking chicanery is at work, but only at the midnight hour. He once asked a boy named Kitchen (no pun intended) and the local vicar who went by the name of Reverend Martin Knowles to attend a feast laid out on one of the tombstones. Reciting the 'De Profundis' as the most appropriate soliloquy for such an occasion, the event was thereafter referred to as the 'Banquet of the Dead'. But when the vicar requested salt for his meal, the Devil and all the food immediately vanished, no doubt returning to the nether world from whence it came.

So if you should decide to test the powers of fate at the midnight hour and challenge his satanic majesty "go always and finally sup with the old gentleman in his abode of darkness". A clear intimation that your soul will be forfeit for acceding to his scurrilous offer. It would appear that sprinkling salt on the old lad's tail is the best method of chasing this fiery denizen back through the portals of Hades. So don't be forgetting to bring the condiments!

Consigned to the older part of the graveyard, behind the church and clearly signposted, is to be found an unusual grave where a small stream runs through the centre of the plot. The story is told of a sea captain who spent more time sailing the oceans of the world than he did at home. His wife was none too pleased with this arrangement and decided that in death they would likewise be parted by water, their bodies to lie either side of the stream. The captain died first and was buried on one side. But when his wife came to join him it was found that the ground was too rocky for excavating a grave and her coffin was placed on top of his. So they ended up united after all but only in the after life.

Investigation of the plethora of fascinating details hereabouts will ensure that at some point the second largest church bell in the country will assail your ears. Weighing

The seafarer's gravestone straddling a minor rill at Kirkby Malham

in at over a ton, 'Big Mike' was cast in 1601 and regularly tolls the passage of time in perfect harmony. With its resonant chime ringing in your ears, amble down to the crossroads, taking advantage of the liquid refreshment on offer at the Victoria Inn should you be so minded. Then cross straight over and go down Green Gate until you reach Hanlith Bridge spanning the River Aire. On its far right, squeeze through a wall gap and go down a short flight of steps to follow the riverbank in a southerly direction.

This section of the walk accompanies the famed Pennine Way. A little after passing through a fence stile, a clear path strikes inland away from the river. Ignore this, sticking close to the water's edge up to a fence gate. The path then crosses open ground when the fence veers away to the left. Rejoin it after 200 metres then slant right across to a footbridge to gain the far side of the river.

Ignore the stile on the right, swinging left up an overgrown patch beside a wall to reach the main road. Go through the gate beside a walled pen, heading right for 100 metres until the start of two paths is reached on the opposite side of the road. Climb an awkwardly stepped wall stile on the left then make a diagonal crossing of the field aiming to the right of the farm.

Over the wall stile, bear right alongside it to a gate, after which the wall is on your left. At the next gate, continue in a straight line over a low knoll and down the opposite slope to a fence stile giving access to the farmyard of Moor End. Pass between the buildings to reach Scosthrop Lane.

Lean right up this for a quarter mile until a gate is reached adjoining a set of sheep pens on the left. Aim half left over the rising field behind and down to a gate on the far side. Then keep right of an old, tree-lined quarry to reach a wall.

After mounting the stile, slant left along the wall then across an open field to the left-hand edge of a wood. Go through a gate to pick up a clear field track that drops down to valley level, circling right at the bottom to pass through a gate. Join a stronger track heading south alongside Otterburn Beck back to the village.

At one time there must have been an abundance of these fascinating creatures splashing about in the water hereabouts. Rarely seen nowadays, one has to question man's impact on the landscape that forces the natural inhabitants into virtual extinction. It has to be admitted that preparation of this volume, however laudable, cannot but exacerbate the problem. What is the answer?

23. Buckden

At the Hub of the Dale

Mysteries: The Blue Lady, GR 926783; Hubberholme's Parliament, GR 926782; Yockenthwaite Circle, GR 900794

Distance Walked: 6 miles

Total Height Climbed: 450 feet, 137 metres

Nearest Shops: Buckden

Start/Finish: At the mouth of Langstrothdale, where the River Wharfe enters the main valley, lies the charming village of Hubberholme. Cross the river by the road bridge opposite the George Inn and park on the riverbank beyond the church.

Terrain: Clear paths all the way with no steep ascents. Mid-level traverse of Langstrothdale on a wide limestone terrace, returning along the riverside.

Map Required: Ordnance Survey 1:25000 Outdoor Leisure 30, Yorkshire Dales Northern & Central areas

Constricted in its upper regions and known as Langstrothdale, the Wharfe valley opens out below the village of Hubberholme, making an abrupt southerly swing. Village is rather an exaggeration for a settlement comprising little more than a pub, farmhouse and church, although it is the latter that deservedly commands the attention of all who pass this way. Being close to the riverbanks it was prone to flooding, one particular inundation resulting in fish swimming amidst the wooden pews. The pews were eventually replaced in 1934 when Robert Thompson of Kilburn was commissioned to refurbish the interior. His trademark was the church mouse, numerous examples of which are carved into the woodwork. So heed the well-intentioned hint whilst exploring the roughcast stone interior that has its origins way back in the 13th century.

A plaque on the wall is dedicated to the celebrated author J.B. Priestley whose ashes were scattered in the churchyard following his death in 1984. His devotion to the Dales was epitomised in Hubberholme, which he held in particular affection.

Whilst strolling around this venerable and ancient pile you might well feel a sense of blue permeating the ether. Perfectly normal if the day beyond these hallowed walls is of the kind we all enjoy, but what if a dark cast hangs low over the fells and the wet stuff is making its damp presence felt?

If such is the case on your visit, then it might well be the Blue Lady who is responsible.

Displaying a centre parting in fair hair drawn tightly back in the manner of early Victorian ladies, this chimera would sit quietly in the front pew before vanishing into the astral plain from whence she emerged. On closer investigation, this ghostly encounter may be explained by a stained-glass window inserted in memory of a vicar's wife from that period.

Could it be that some traumatic event in their lives prompted these appearances? This is a tantalising enigma to mull over whilst wandering over to the old vicarage at the far side of the river. In the 18th century Hubberholme had to share its reli-

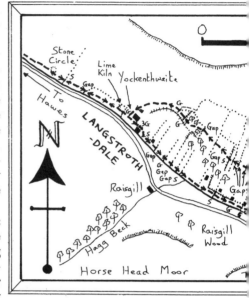

gious needs with the more permanent chapel at Halton Gill over the fell in Littondale. One of the longest serving curates was a Mr Lindley who conducted services at Hubberholme between 1802 and 1833.

But it was not always possible to make the trip every Sunday, especially when Horse Head Pass became blocked with snowdrifts in winter. In his later years the ageing preacher rode a white horse across the fell. Down in Hubberholme, a hawk-eyed lookout standing on a rooftop heralded his approach with the cry of, "T' minister's comin'". The bell would then be tolled to bring the faithful together.

The old vicarage is now the George Inn where a tradition has long been enacted every New Year that involves the letting of land to help the poor of the parish. Accompanied by much merry making and copious consumption of the amber nectar, the ceremony began with a church service, after which all parties retired to the inn where the vicar and churchwardens assumed the role of the 'House of Lords'. Below in the bar the farmers became the 'House of Commons', as they were the ones doing the bidding. The 'Poor Pasture' was a sixteen-acre plot behind the inn, the lucky recipient being allowed to catch rabbits in addition to grazing his animals. Once the final bids were accepted, the vicar would decide how the money was to be spent and "a right grand do was had by all".

So if you should chance to do this walk around New Year, find out when

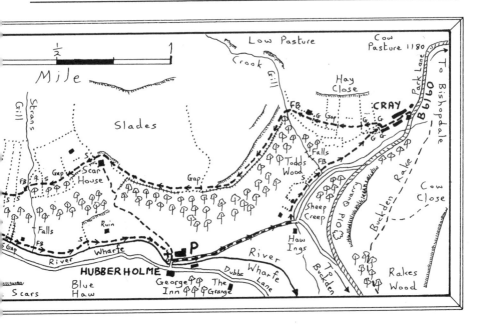

the ceremony is being conducted and join in the fun as an honorary 'member of parliament'. This fine walk should naturally be enjoyed prior to the festivities so walk up the old road past the church for half a mile until a footpath signpost is reached pointing the way to Cray.

Go through the gate on your left and accompany Cray Gill upstream on a clear trail through the lower pastures. Notice the unique building methods adopted for the construction of drystone walls – it is displayed on the end piece that is soon passed. After nudging two wall ends the path surges ahead for 200 metres to mount a stile, continuing over rock slabs enclosed within the sylvan glen.

Once the footbridge spanning Crook Gill is crossed, the way climbs away from the gill up an open grass slope. At the top end it veers towards a gate in the wall and into a short, walled corridor at the edge of Cray hamlet. Once through the gate at the end, swing sharply to the left through another gate, doubling back to head west across the enclosed middle pasture of Hay Close.

A wall gate followed by a gap will find you approaching a prominent barn. Go through the gate, keeping to the left of the barn, then bend right into the deep cutting eroded by Crook Gill. Cross the tree-lined gill by a sturdy footbridge, thereafter leaning left to accompany a fence skirting the upper limits of Todd's Wood.

There follows a leisurely stroll along the broad terrace sandwiched between exposed bands of limestone scarring. Having passed through a wall gap, take the time to pause and cast your peepers to the south where the classical symmetry of Wharfedale's glacial origins is displayed to perfection. Then continue with the broad right-hand sweep into Langstrothdale until stepped limestone layers are negotiated above Scar House.

A remote house high on the northern flank of the dale, it was a secret meeting place for Quakers back in the 17th century when this Nonconformist sect was savagely persecuted for its faith. George Fox, the founder of the movement, is known to have stayed at Scar House on two occasions, the second in 1677, the night after his sojourn at Countersett (See Walk 9). At the side of the current building (dating from the 19th century) in a small walled enclosure is the Quaker burial ground.

After crossing the fell track, go through a gate followed soon after by a gap in a broken wall, still maintaining the same height. The path then enters a small copse by a stile and leaves by a footbridge. We then bear left down a sharp embankment, continuing on a lower terrace. A number of long, narrow fields are now crossed. Counting them off as follows should bring you to the final wall gap at the upper corner of open woodland: two stiles, four gaps, one fence stile and yet another gap.

We continue our descent of the valley side to reach a fence and accompany this along a level section through a fence gate to the end of the tree growth. Pass through the gate to join a fell track dropping down to the farming enclave of Yockenthwaite. Unless time has caught up with those having an urgent appointment with their tax inspector, there is no excuse for a direct return to Hubberholme along the riverside.

Instead, bear right to follow the River Wharfe upstream for half a mile to visit one of the few Neolithic stone circles still intact within the Yorkshire Dales. After passing through the first gate, take note of the fine example of a limekiln on the right of the path. Stroll on for a quarter mile through a wall gap. Beyond the next stile is the stone circle to the right of the path. Once thought to have religious significance connected with Druid rituals and ceremonies based on the worship of the sun, it has also been suggested that they are burial mounds. Quite possibly they were the first form of calendar, being astronomical observatories through which the major seasons of the year were tracked by means of the sun and star movements. Great moments in the passage of time could then be noted.

In truth, their real purpose remains a mystery that still perplexes archaeologists, and that is one of their unfailing attractions. One thing they do tell us is where centres of population gathered in prehistoric times. And clearly, Langstrothdale was one of these.

Having determined your own solution to the problem, turn around and retrace your steps back to Yockenthwaite. Continue along the side of the river to Hubberholme in company with the Dales Way, emerging on the lane adjacent to the church. A verbose description of this obvious route is unnecessary if you take heed of the map. In actuality, there is no other way to go except down the constricted valley.

Arriving at the rear of the church, pass through a gate and down a wall passage to the road by the bridge spanning the Wharfe. Then its left back to the car and the termination of a splendid round that visits the entire breadth of human settlement in Upper Wharfedale from prehistoric times to the present. Together with a glimpse into the ethereal world from which legends derive, this is a walk to remember.

The origins of stone circles like this one in Langstrothdale are shrouded in mystery

24. Arncliffe
Vision from the Cauldron

Mystery: The Wise Old Woman, GR 732718

Distance Walked: 10 miles

Total Height Climbed: 1100 feet, 335 metres

Start/Finish: There should be no problem parking in Arncliffe. But to avoid cluttering up the area around the village green, stick to the pull-in at the north-west end, adjacent to Cowside Beck.

Terrain: Wild and lonely moorland plateau between limestone 'clouds'. Clear paths most of the way.

Nearest Shops: Tea rooms and a post office at Arncliffe but more variety at Kettlewell.

Map Required: Ordnance Survey 1:25000 Outdoor Leisure 2, Yorkshire Dales South and West areas

A merdale, Vendale and Beckindale – take your pick! These are all alternative renditions of the name that have been applied to one of the most appealing villages to grace this most wild and romantic of National Parks. Arncliffe has been eulogised in poetic verse by William Wordsworth in his 'White Doe of Rylstone' and Charles Kingsley, following a visit, included the settlement in his renowned Water Babies. Even the popular soap 'Emmerdale' was initially based here prior to its removal to the current purpose-built site.

All reasons enough for correctly supposing that this village nestling below "the cliff of the eagles" is definitely worth more than just a cursory glance. Littondale has quite clearly not been content to play second fiddle to its larger neighbour Wharfdale. Perhaps because it has been in continuous occupation since the Stone Age and is accessible at both ends as well as in mid-course where Arncliffe developed.

Although the present church is of recent origin, a church is known to have existed on its present site adjoining the River Skirfare since Saxon times, followed later by one erected by the Normans. The Battle of Flodden Field, which took place in the reign of Henry VIII, recruited fighting men from the village whose names are listed on a parchment scroll within the church.

Oldest inhabitants of all are those who chose to live in the caves below Blue Scar, either for protection or seclusion. Weapons and coins were found in these primitive abodes, which later provided a refuge for wolves until the animals were driven to extinction in the 14th century.

Take a stroll around the village at some period during your visit. The main group of houses faces the village green, with its now redundant water pump in the middle. Like a miniature belfry, it merely adds to the quintessential allure emanating from this most attractive of villages. One of the cottages, although which one remains a mystery in itself, is said to be where 'The Wise Woman of Littondale' conducted her nefarious business of healing and astrological predictions. One of the earliest practitioners of alternative medicine maybe? Strange rituals that were at the time closely reminiscent of witchcraft earned her a solid reputation and those needing assistance actively sought her out.

So-called witches were often reclusive old women who did much good in their communities. It is a sad indictment of human nature that they are the first to be blamed when disasters occur. On one particular occasion a sceptic arrived to challenge Bertha's claim that she could predict future events. Taking up the proffered gauntlet, she mixed up a potent brew comprising all manner of quirky ingredients in her steaming cauldron. And muttering the prescribed incantation she told the man to stare into the foaming pot, where he was amazed to see a close friend looking decidedly ill at ease.

Realising that Bertha was no scheming impostor, the man agreed to her

A ghostly past adds to the disturbing aura surrounding Arncliffe Bridge, especially at midnight

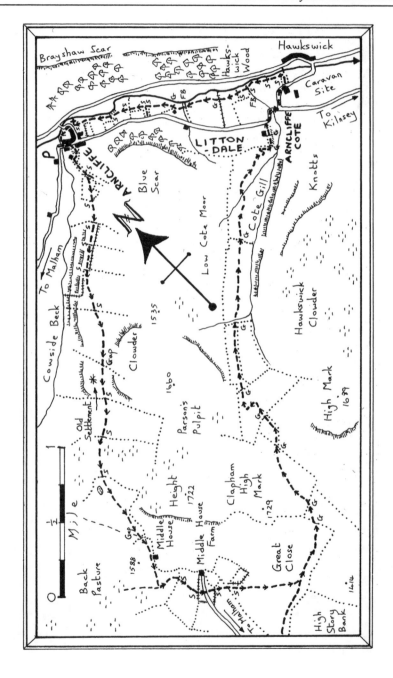

suggestion that he visit Arncliffe Bridge at midnight alone, where the final act of this bizarre episode would be played out. This he duly did but all he noted was a low moaning sound and slight disturbance of the waters beneath the bridge. Nothing else happened so he returned to his father's cottage – followed by a large black dog that vanished as quickly as it had appeared.

Relating this incident to the old woman next day, she informed him that the dog was a barguest or emissary of the nether world and not of mortal descent. Its presence denoted an imminent death. But when and who would be the victim? Three hours later, the man learned that his friend had committed suicide at the very spot where the river disturbance had occurred on the previous night.

In view of these bewitching elements surrounding the bridge at Arncliffe, prudence dictates that we visit the site at the end of our walk. So take the narrow walled lane to the right of The Falcon Inn and follow it up towards the steeply shelving western flank of the valley. Watch for a stile on the right then slant across the adjacent field, nudging a wall corner to reach the next stile above and close to a corner. The clear path continues to climb, soon reaching a stile. Beyond this is a fence on the left. Levelling out, our route keeps above the lines of white scarring that characterise the landscape hereabouts along the enclosed valley of Cowbeck.

Known as the Monk's Road, it was clearly used by our cowled cousins of yesteryear who were in the habit of travelling between Arncliffe and Malham. One can only speculate as to whether they fell prey to the bands of wolves that roamed these wild moors.

Following two more stiles, the fence changes to the right, albeit briefly, after which the path veers left away from the main valley, crossing an area of limestone hillocks known as Clowder. Their association with the bands of cumulus that frequent this undulating moorland is unquestioned. Homing into a side valley, the path enters National Trust land passing close to an ancient Brigantean encampment. Such a far-flung setting must have been chosen with security in mind. For who else but those in fear of their lives would volunteer to inhabit this bleak and cheerless plateau, except, of course, the wandering wolves?

Easy to follow, the path selects the best route that meanders between exposed patios of limestone pavement, eventually approaching civilisation. After crossing a broken wall followed immediately by a prominent signpost pointing the way to Darnbrook, we approach Middle House. Keep to the right of this abandoned farmstead, accompanying the enclosing wall until it slips away to the left.

Another 100 metres will bring you to a T-junction where you should head left along this major fell track to reach a wall. Mount the ladder stile then stroll down the grass slope beyond to a fence stile giving on to the access road serving Middle House Farm where Oliver Cromwell once stayed (See Walk 22). Cross straight over this concrete ribbon and aim for the left-hand corner of the adjoining grass sward.

Mount the stile and bear half left over to the next stile in a wall. You will now be entering the broad, open tract of Great Close, an undulating pasture sprinkled with white rocks like giant hailstones. Slant away from the wall on the right, heading south-east for a half mile until you merge with another major track that links Malham and Littondale. Stroll up East Great Close to pass through a gate at the top end. Cut across the field corner to another gate then up the facing grassy rake of Clapham High Mark. On passing through the next gate, accompany a broken wall on the right around to the gate at the end. This brings us to the highest point on the walk at 1650ft (503 metres).

Our route now drops down into the depression that marks the source of Cote Gill. Watch for the emphatic zigzag marked by signposts that will see you approaching a wall gate at the lower level on the left side of the newly emergent watercourse. The clear track will lead you down the gentle gradient of this north-west flank above Cote Gill in stark contrast to the cliffs of limestone on the opposite side of this deeply cut valley. The rising tiers of exposed scarring behind are aptly named Hawkswick Clowder.

On reaching the lower intake wall the path makes an abrupt switch left then right to pass through a double gate before entering a constricted passage down to Arncliffe Cote. Go through the farmyard and down the access to head right along the valley road. After the 'dogleg' bend, stroll quickly past the entrance to Hawkswick Caravan Site, the very same that struck the eye with the force of a rampant rhino as we descended Cote Moor. At the T-junction, bear left until an enclosed track is reached on the left. Go down it but do not cross the footbridge spanning the river. Instead mount a stile on the left and take the riverside path back to Arncliffe. Initially fenced in, it soon opens out to cross the fields, leaning away from the river once a small footbridge is crossed.

Keep with this grassy trail until a major tributary is negotiated by another footbridge. Then lean half right past a barn and through a gate to gain the next field. Bear right, away from the wall on your left to a narrow field access track stiled at either side. Accompany the continuing wall to the end of the field. After this stile, cross a short stretch to rejoin the riverbank by some trees and a wall. Stick with the river all the way into Arncliffe, passing through a stile to enter a farmyard.

Amble down past the church to the road. Approach Arncliffe Bridge with trepidation in view of the macabre events that occurred beneath the stone arches. Then follow a rough track that passes behind the cottages fronting the green. Circle round to accompany Cowside Beck back to the north end of the village.

25. Grassington
'G' is for ...Gibbet

Mystery: Tom Lee – Doctor Killer, GR 003641

Distance Walked: 5 miles

Total Height Climbed: 350 feet, 107 metres

Start/Finish: Make use of the official car park to the south of Grassington. After crossing the River Wharfe, follow the B6265 around until a car park sign indicates a right turning.

Terrain: A beautiful riverside walk on limestone surrenders to the enclosed forest where some upward perambulation is required.

Nearest Shops: Grassington

Map Required: Ordnance Survey 1:25000 Outdoor Leisure 2, Yorkshire Dales Southern & Western areas

Although a fine village oozing charm and character and flaunting an ancient pedigree, Grassington is not the sort of place one should seek out if the idea is to 'get away from it all'. A popular honeypot, its narrow streets attract legions of sightseers and on a busy weekend are literally choked with visitors. This walk does, however, attempt to escape the throngs and in this respect is hugely successful.

But can Grassington in reality only be classed as a village? Certainly it boasts a town hall and was granted a town charter back in 1282 enabling a fair and market to be held. And today it houses the offices of the Yorkshire Dales National Park authority, further enhancing its status in the South Dales region. There has been a settlement here since Iron Age times from around 300BC and the extensive primitive field system can still be made out on the hill slopes to the north of this large village, or is it a small town?

Vestiges of the lead-mining industry dating back to Roman occupation and an important source of prosperity well into the 19th century are still visible today. Definitely, Grassington is worthy of more than just a cursory glance but save your explorations for the end of the walk. First, make your way down to Grassington Bridge where the famous gibbet used to be erected, a gruesome discouragement for any local hotheads considering a life of crime. Here it was that a certain Tom Lee of Grassington made criminal history by having three charges of murder placed against him for killing the same man.

Once the village blacksmith, he is remembered by a plaque on the wall of

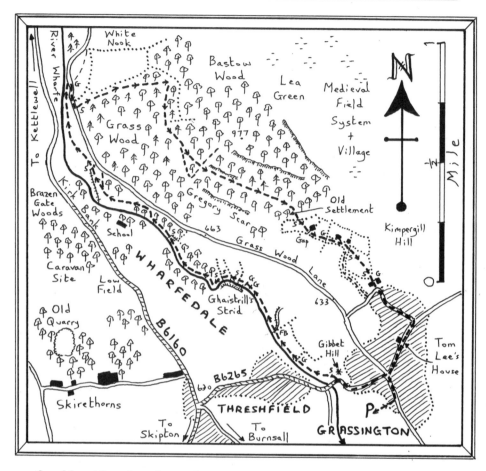

the old smithy where he conducted his business on the main street. Now an artist's showroom, it recalls an indolent fellow who was more in tune with the clink of ale tankards at the inn managed by his wife than the clang of hammer on anvil. Also regarded as a bully and brawler, Tom Lee's lazy attitude led to pecuniary embarrassment that often meant the finger of suspicion pointing unerringly in his direction when burglaries occurred. But there was never sufficient evidence to convict the rascally braggart. Continued monetary worries led the blacksmith to seriously consider robbing the messenger who regularly delivered the lead miners' wages.

In the 18th century, 200 men were employed in the mines littering the landscape around Grassington, which meant a substantial payroll. Unfortunately for Tom, his effort to remove the wage sack was stymied by a vigilant guardian who also managed to put a bullet in his shoulder. Badly wounded, Lee sought the assistance of Dr. Petty in Grassington, who promised not to report the incident to the authorities if Tom would mend his ways. This he duly did, and life settled down to a period of normality. But Tom Lee knew that one word from the doctor and he would be arrested. Over the next few months his fears grew into an obsession until he realised that there was only one course left open.

As the only doctor serving Upper Wharfedale, the good medic often travelled along lonely trails to the outlying communities. Once when returning from Conistone, he was accosted by Lee close to the top end of Grass Wood. Bludgeoned and badly beaten, he was left for dead. Lee returned home, himself bruised and bloody from the encounter. After learning her husband's foul deed, his wife insisted he return to the scene of the crime and bury the body so that the heinous attack could not be traced back to him.

Tom's apprentice, a lad called Bowness, overheard their plans and was forced to implicate himself by assisting in their grisly venture. Everybody suspected Tom Lee but nothing could be proved until, eventually, Bowness returned from Durham where he had gone to work and confessed his part in the gruesome proceedings. This was enough to ensure that the blacksmith danced a merry jig at the end of a rope on the 25 July 1768. After his body had been left to rot on what locals termed 'Dark Corner', the chains were said to have been interred within the foundations of the new stone bridge that now crosses the Wharfe.

Controversy still exists as to where exactly the chained body of Tom Lee was displayed. Some claim it was in Grass Wood near to the deadly spot. I prefer the version above related to me by a local farmer whilst sitting on a bench at that very same place where the rattling of chains and ghostly appearances have been reported.

From Dark Corner, pass through a stile and amble down to the riverside before heading upstream. After a half mile, the river is squeezed between outcrops of limestone forming a fearsome set of rapids known as Ghaistrill's Strid. 'Strid' is a common word in Wharfedale to describe this caustic turbulence in the natural flow of the river. At this point the path climbs above the river, being pinched by a fence. Beyond the final wall stile, return to the riverbank where the path swings between trees.

Keep going upstream to mount a fence stile, after which the river flows through a short gorge with dense woodland on either side. The trail now climbs above the river into the trees, eventually making a gradual descent to the lower level as the tree cover terminates. Continue round the edge of the trees to clear a fence stile and head out on to the flat, grassy flood plain. Maintain a direction due north between the river and Grass Wood Lane until the path reaches a gate. Bear right back up the lane for 150 metres then

The chains used to hang Tom Lee are supposedly interred in the foundations of Grassington Bridge

plunge left over a stile into the gloomy confines of Grass Wood. Ascend the main track until it bends sharply to the right. This is the approximate site where Tom Lee despatched the hapless Dr. Petty to a permanent appointment in that great surgery in the sky.

The tree cover was completely different in those times with fewer walls and more open countryside. Coniferous growth that took a hold of the original woodland is gradually being cut back and replaced by less claustrophobic varieties to encourage the spread of undergrowth. Keep following this main path as it continues uphill before dropping down to pass an ancient archaeological site on the periphery.

Emerging from the woods, cross a short grassy sward, keeping right of a barn through a gap. Stroll along the broad, walled corridor and through the gate at the end, after which Cove Lane is much narrower. At the first bend to the right keep ahead over a corner stile, crossing to the far side of the adjacent field. Mount a stile and walk down to a gate opening into a farmyard.

This marks the start of Grassington's built-up area. Stroll down to a crossroads and hang right down the steepening main street, keeping a watchful eye open for Tom Lee's old smithy. Exploration of the multifarious nooks and crannies that comprise the village/town will complete a walk where beauty and the beast go hand in hand.

26. Threshfield
All's Well by the Wharfe

Mysteries: Lady Well, GR 998637; Pam the Fiddler, GR 997634

Distance Walked: 4 miles

Total Height Climbed: 100 feet, 31 metres

Start/Finish: Parking in Threshfield is limited to side roads off the B6265. Approaching from the west, make use of a modern development down the cul-de-sac known as Piece Fields on the right opposite the village store.

Terrain: Rolling grass pastures interfaced with drystone walls. Care is needed when crossing the River Wharfe by means of the stepping stones.

Nearest Shops: Threshfield

Map Required: Ordnance Survey 1:25000 Outdoor Leisure 2, Yorkshire Dales Southern & Western areas

Due in no small measure to its limestone base, the Wharfe valley is renowned for the abundance of its wells and springs – essential features in the past when a reliable source of water encouraged a settled population to grow and flourish. In those far off times before the invention of hygiene, much of the water supply that people regularly imbibed was contaminated with sewage and waste matter. So when a source was discovered that did not make them ill, it was a just cause for celebration. Such sources were often dedicated to saints on account of their purity and many were thought to have mystical powers with the ability to cure all manner of ailments.

Today we view them as quirky facets of the rural landscape, not appreciating their importance to our medieval forebears when the piped water we take for granted was still many centuries away. Pagan rituals surrounding the 'life-giving' properties attached to wells eventually gave way to Christian veneration. The most significant local well is close to Grassington Bridge, beside the River Wharfe.

So walk down the hill from Threshfield and turn right by Ladywell Cottage. Immediately beyond on the left is a narrow ginnel leading down to the well, which has become a religious shrine. What a stark contrast to its past association as a refuge from impish boggarts and roguish goblins. One incident relates to a local man returning home from a drinking session in a Grassington hostelry and witnessing a group of fairies dancing in a field. A fit of sneezing caused the surprised fairies to glimpse the inebriated chap

'Pam the Fiddler' was headmaster of Threshfield School

spying on them from behind a wall. Angry at this invasion of their privacy, they instantly gave chase.

The panic-stricken fugitive dashed down to Lady Well and jumped in, knowing that he would be safe during the hours of darkness. And there he remained, up to his neck in the cold water, until morning. Unable to breach the liquid cordon, the little people could only stamp and fume on the bank in impotent fury at having been bested.

At sunrise, they finally departed with a dire warning of retribution should the bedraggled man ever trespass on their ritual in the future. Even though none the worse for his damp experience, the poor chap had learned a salutary lesson that was duly emphasised by the acid tongue of his waspish spouse when he finally arrived home. Peering into the well, it is clear that considerable infilling has occurred since that time. Today, even a dog would be hard pressed to fully immerse itself in the placid waters. Many pilgrims still come here to escape the traumas of contemporary life and to seek a brief period of solitary reflection. So perhaps these two views of Lady Well and others of similar ilk are not so conflicting after all.

Having duly paid your respects at the well, continue south down the road for a quarter mile until you reach the primary school on the right. A fine example of Stuart architecture, it was built in 1674 as a free grammar school, relinquishing this status in 1870 – but not the resident ghost.

Pam the Fiddler (a man, incidentally) is known to have frightened teachers and mesmerised the pupils with his hypnotic playing. This particular

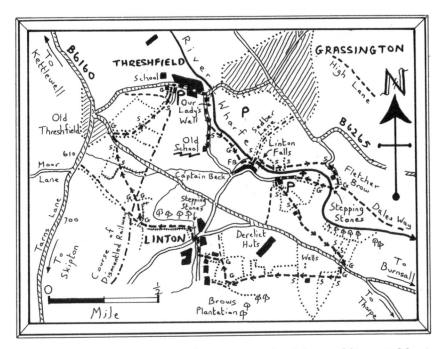

spectre was a past headmaster who entertained at fairs, weddings and festivals throughout the locality with his violin. One night, following a particularly blithe event and rather an excessive consumption of the amber nectar, Pam sat outside the school where he lived merrily fiddling to the stars.

The local rector was none too pleased at this blatant and rather noisy display of conviviality, him being an austere and humourless sort. Remonstrations for the fiddler to cease his playing proved fruitless and a fight ensued which left Pam dead on the ground. Although distraught at the result of his over-zealous actions, the cleric was secure in his own mind that it had been a fair fight. Having soothed his conscience and regained his composure, the virulent vicar had no intention of confessing his crime to the authorities and proceeded to bury Pam's corpse near the school.

Even today, a stroll by this macabre site after dark might well result in you hearing the plaintive lilt of a violin floating on the breeze. Or maybe it's just an evening concert at the primary school.

Returning down the road, take the footpath signposted on the right along the riverbank. Opposite the weir, go through a gate and across an open stretch of grass to reach a neat, stone footbridge spanning the minor tributary of Captain Beck. Over this, swing left along a passage behind some houses to gain the main footbridge across the Wharfe.

The tale is told of certain local lad called Billy who late one night was crossing the bridge following a drinking session in Grassington after a re-nowned event known as the clock-dressing ceremony. Claiming to be in full possession of his faculties (don't they all), the young chap said he felt something brush past him with rattling chains, but could see nothing. The noise kept following him and he realised it must be the infamous Grassington Barguest, which followed him across the river all the way back to his house. He then caught sight of the thing – described as a great woolly creature like a huge sheep. Angry and more than a little afraid, he berated the beast, shouting at it to be gone, but with no response. The barguest re-mained where it was.

All this noise roused his slumbering wife who came down and opened the door, whereupon the beast departed. The man later announced that, "This thing gat up an' walked off – for it war more fear'd o't' wife than it war o' me!" Neither of them saw the barguest again. This is a fine story to con-template as you gaze upon the awesome power of Linton Falls command-ing attention downstream.

Intricately moulded, the limestone bedrock creates its own Impression-ist landscape that is just as startling as the cascading foam of the river. On the far side of the Wharfe continue downstream, soon mounting two wall stiles before slanting away left to gain the back lane serving Fletcher Brow. Head right past the house and along a walled corridor to a gate at the end. The well-known and much-frequented Dales Way continues onward as we swing right down to the riverside and a marvellous set of stepping stones. Easily 50 metres wide at this point, the flat boulders should allow you to straddle the river dry-footed. A rousing prospect not to be missed.

On the far shore, head upstream over a grass tract to a gate giving access to the churchyard of St Michael and All Angels. Squat and insignificant from the outside, it boasts an ancient heritage and provides an important function as the parish church for the villages around. Pass through to the access road, noting the free car park on the left for future visits. Amble down the road until you reach Holme House on the left then go up the little used track at the side. Mount a stile at the end and make a diagonal crossing of the field to another stile at the far side. Keeping left of a stone lathe, lean right around a low knoll to follow a thin trod in the grass.

The path stays above a clutch of trees and negotiates two wall stiles to reach a gate giving onto the Burnsall road. On the far side, offset to the right, is a gate. Walk up beside a wall on your right to a corner round which a stile is mounted, allowing you to head due west. Over the next stile, keep right of a substantial lathe to pass above two distinctive wells. The old one, now re-duced to an exposed clutter of rocks, has been superseded by a newer ef-fort, the sides of which are concrete-lined for preservation and use by the animals. Straddle two more wall stiles to pass right of a collection of dilapi-dated hutments. An old army camp perhaps?

The path then leans slightly left, chaperoning a wall along to a corner. Flick right through a newish gate and follow the wall until a broken section is reached. Now cut half right over to the far corner where a gate brings you to an old lane. The original right of way keeps forward but is much overgrown so heave a left along a farm track to reach the main street of Linton.

Reckoned by some to be the prettiest village in Wharfedale, why stop at one valley? This enchanting settlement could easily claim to be amongst the premiere contenders for such an honour in the whole of the National Park – and beyond. All the requisite ingredients are present – babbling brook, ancient packhorse bridge, leafy arbours, stepping stones, picturesque cottages and a blue-ribbon country pub.

Bear right past the youth hostel, noting the poignant verse that clearly indicates that 'Holiday Fellowship' is firmly in agreement with these sentiments:

> *'Friend when you stay, or sit or take your ease*
> *On moor or fell or under spreading trees*
> *Pray leave no traces of your wayside meal*
> *No paper bag no scattered orange peel*
> *Nor daily journal littered on the grass*
> *Others may view these with distaste and pass.*
> *Let no one say it and say it to your shame*
> *That all was beauty here until you came.'*

On reaching the B6265, turn left over the bridge spanning Linton Beck then immediately right along a narrow passage hemmed in by undergrowth. A classic set of stepping stones gives access to a house on the opposite side, after which the enclosed path bends round to the left and eventually arrives at a gate. Go through this and along a fence, keeping left of some trees to pass beneath the old railway line that is now dismantled and gated at either side. Thereafter, lean half right across an open field to a fence corner 200 metres distant. A plank bridge and stile allow passage over Ings Beck, a tributary of Captain Beck. Keep ahead up a slight incline to reach the B6160.

Head left for 100 metres, crossing over the road and taking a gated track. At the end of this walled corridor, mount a stile to accompany the wall on your left to the end of the field and another stile. Beyond this, notice the nature conservation trackway heading left **but** keep straight on, following a narrow path behind the new housing of Piece Fields. Two gates at the end bring us back to Threshfield's main street.

This area used to be the terminus of the railway line from Skipton – no trace of which can now be seen. Threshfield was the end of the line that brought tourists into Wharfedale and ferried lead ore out. Today's railway serves only the large Swinden limestone quarry located just north of Cracoe.

27. Rylstone

Deer Emily

Mystery: The Rylstone Doe, GR 972588

Distance Walked: 7½ miles

Total Height Climbed: 500 feet, 152 metres

Start/Finish: Heading north up the B6265 from the direction of Skipton, turn right at Rylstone and park on the broad verge adjacent to the church.

Terrain: Rolling grass pastures enclosed by stone walls contrast with the wild and lonely heather-clad moorlands.

Nearest Shops: Cracoe

Map Required: Ordnance Survey 1:25000 Outdoor Leisure 2, Yorkshire Dales Southern & Western areas

Like many parish churches, St Peter's at Rylstone was rebuilt in the 19th century (1852 to be precise) and the plans of the old building can be viewed inside the present edifice. The final resting place of the graveyard's most celebrated guest, however, appears to have disappeared into obscurity. A search of the wide array of tombstones failed to reveal the final resting place of Emily Norton, buried here some four centuries ago. Neither does anything remain of Rylstone Hall where the Norton Family resided, the exception being the raised embankments that enclosed the 'fish ponds'.

Set amongst a collection of dispersed cottages, the church at Rylstone is easily missed, being set back from the main road. Some authorities claim the view from the church tower is one of the finest in the Dales, a difficult opinion to contest as the church remains locked outside working hours. As firm followers of the established church, the Nortons doubtless chose the adjoining site for their manor house on religious grounds rather than for the quality of the panorama.

Apart from Francis Norton, who opted to follow the breakaway concept of the Anglican Church instigated by Henry VIII, the Nortons remained staunch followers of Catholicism. Their involvement in the rebellion known as 'The Rising of the North' led to the arrest and execution of the ringleaders. Due to his Anglican affiliation, Francis alone survived. But not for long! Regarded by the 'faithful' as a traitor, he was set upon and murdered, his body being interred in Bolton Priory. This left Emily as the sole remaining member of the Norton family, whose lands were confiscated by the Crown and handed over to the loyal Cliffords.

To keep her company, little Emily acquired a young white doe that

Emily Norton is said to be buried in the graveyard at Rylstone church

would follow her around wherever she went. When it became fully grown, she released it into the wild to join the herd of deer foraging on Burnsall Moor. Alone in the world now that her family were all gone, she wandered aimlessly up and down Wharfedale seeking shelter from Catholic sympathisers.

Some years later, whilst revisiting her old home at Rylstone, Emily, now a young woman, rested against an oak tree, whereupon that very same doe detached itself from the herd and trotted over to greet its old mistress. The trusting nature of an animal traditionally known for its timid and shy character came to the attention of William Wordsworth some three centuries later. He immortalised the story of the white doe of Rylstone in his epic poem, which extolled the lady's affection for the elegant creature thus:

> *'The pleading look the lady viewed,*
> *And, by her gushing thoughts subdued,*
> *She melted in tears -*
> *A flood of tears that flowed apace,*
> *Upon the happy creature's face.'*

As the years marched ever onward, Emily spent more time at Bolton Priory praying at the graveside of her relatives, accompanied of course by the faithful doe (See Walk 30). When eventually her own heavenly appointment was announced, she was buried at Rylstone. The doe continued its

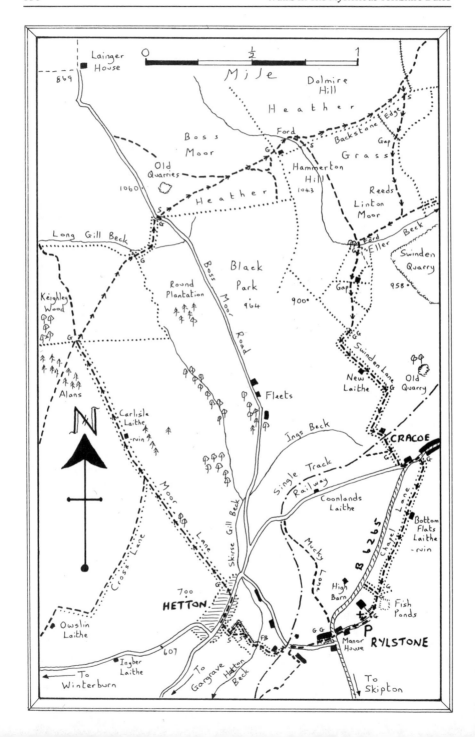

visits to the priory but also came to Rylstone Church every Sunday, much to the amazement of the congregation. And they continued to be thus honoured until the white doe eventually departed for that great deer park in the sky. Years later, Emily and her four-legged friend were immortalised at Townley Hall near Burnley whose inhabitants were similarly loyal to the Catholic faith through that dark era of persecution.

From St Peter's Church, stroll down to the B6265 and go straight over to join the old bridleway to Kilnsey. The turnpike road from Cracoe to Skipton replaced this ancient trackway in 1852, although many farmers and hauliers still used the high-level route in the shadow of Norton Tower that rejoined the new road at Sandy Beck House. This piece of chicanery was done to avoid paying the road toll when the price was doubled.

A certain Jamie Ibbotson of Threshfield, and clearly not a member of the pauper class, devised his own method of avoiding payment at the tollhouse. He would present a £50 note, knowing that the toll keeper would have no change and be obliged to let him through free of charge.

After passing the duck pond, once the village green, a pair of gates allow passage through the yards serving local houses before merging with the lane to Hetton. Bear right under the railway bridge then hard left alongside it, following a narrow, walled corridor when it bends right past Burton House. Follow this pleasant path around to cross Hetton Beck on a solid footbridge then go up the far side of the shallow depression for 150 metres only. Watch for a stile on the left that affords a half right crossing of the adjoining field. This short cut will return you to the original path through a gap stile, thence continuing ahead to meet the road through Hetton village.

Take a right along the main street, past the pub and Methodist church where the conflicting aims of temperance and the demon drink now exist side by side in relative harmony. Slant left up Moor Lane, which is a walled track, pursuing an arrow-straight course for 1½ miles until a gate is reached giving access to the open fell above Winterburn Reservoir – it can be seen below on the left. Our way forks half right across rough moorland until the path slants in to meet a wall, followed soon after by a gate.

Now entering a walled corridor, we continue along this meandering continuation of Moor Lane to a gate at its terminus. Now turn right down Boss Moor Lane for no more than 50 metres before mounting a fence stile on the opposite side of the road. Maintaining a general north-easterly bearing towards Wharfedale, the thin trod picks a delicate trail across the tussocky heather expanse, assisted by a line of marker posts.

After a quarter of a mile our narrow path forks into a major fell track now used primarily by shooting parties, Boss Moor having become well established with grouse coveys. When this track swings to the right, keep straight on along a grassy course aiming for a gate in the wall ahead. The path now makes a gradual descent to ford the upper reaches of Hammerton Hill Sike.

A short cut now presents itself for those sad souls frightened off by the remote nature of the terrain. It heads right over a ladder stile then follows the stream down to a small copse. Far better to continue over the rising knoll in front, where the path sticks close to the wall cresting Backstone Edge. To the left a wilderness of heather lifts gently on to Threshfield Moor.

Once the Edge has been topped watch for a stile in the wall on your right. It is located 50 metres short of a fence at the end through which this track continues. At the far side of the wall, lean half right to head south over pathless ground. Beyond this short hummocky section, drop down to the point where a fence and wall meet. Go through the gap, circling left as the wall heads down towards Eller Beck.

Immediately in front across the depression and largely hidden from view is the enormous Swinden Quarry. The rail branch line from Skipton that once terminated at Threshfield is now used specifically for exporting the limestone. Keep above the dry reed-choked gully, following a thin trail that soon veers away right and wanders down to merge with a clearer track that parallels Eller Beck.

Head right, upstream, towards a small copse of trees. Here the beck is easily forded. Climb out of the cutting through a wall gate, followed soon after by a gap. Once in the rough field south of the wood, aim to reach the far wall 20 metres to the right of a new barn. Ignore the red herring that will deposit you in the wrong field, instead striking out across reedy ground on a thin trod.

Pass through a gap in the wall, leaning left down to a wall corner then continuing down to the bottom left corner of the field. From the other side of a small, enclosed square with two gates, amble down the zigzagged course of this walled track known as Swinden Lane. Stick with it all the way to the main road, passing under a railway bridge and through two more gates en route.

Bear left along the B6265 for 150 metres before crossing the road and going through a gate into Chapel Lane. Once the original road used by all and sundry before it was replaced in 1852, it now offers an easy return to Rylstone for walkers. Prior to reaching the new farmstead built on the foundations of Rylstone Hall, go through a pair of gates to pass the 'fish pond'. Now drained, there is little evidence of the scaly swimmers that once cavorted inside this excavated hollow.

On the fellside behind, a war memorial and cross dominate the horizon. Another gate brings us to the farm access road. So cross straight over to accompany the ancient pathway beside the church back to the car. On a Sunday do not be surprised to see white creatures nuzzling at the grass around the tombstones in the churchyard. Observant walkers will soon realise that these are, in fact, sheep and not relatives of the celebrated White Doe of Rylstone.

28. Up the Pole!

Burnsall

Mystery: The Elusive Maypole, GR 032611; Elbolton Cave, GR 008615
Distance Walked: 5½ miles
Total Height Climbed: 1050 feet, 320 metres
Start/Finish: Make use of the official car park in Burnsall – located on the west side of the River Wharfe, downstream from the bridge.
Terrain: A dense mosaic of walled fields in the Wharfe valley surrenders to wild moorland of bilberry and heather.
Nearest Shops: Burnsall
Map Required: Ordnance Survey 1:25000 Outdoor Leisure 2, Yorkshire Dales South and West

Flanking a wide meander of the River Wharfe on its west bank, the village of Burnsall has grown up at one of the few crossing points that have been bridged. Typically moulded in the style that we have come to expect from villages in the Yorkshire Dales, it boasts an ancient pedigree stretching back to Saxon times.

Harking back to a bygone age, at village celebrations local folk dance round the maypole and enjoy a splendid day with visitors coming from far and wide to take part in the festivities. One day many years ago some of those visitors hailed from nearby Thorpe. So impressed were they by the fine specimen gracing the village green that they were determined to have one of their own. And what better place to obtain it than Burnsall itself? A few days later, after the excitement had died down, these sneaky rogues returned to snaffle the maypole, re-erecting it at Thorpe. Searching high and low, the Burnsall villagers were unable to locate the missing item. But they had failed to include Thorpe in their quest due to its obscure locale. Eventually, however, it was spotted by shepherds from the fells over which our walk proceeds.

A substantial retinue of stout-hearted young men marched on Thorpe and easily retrieved the stolen object, repositioning it in its rightful place on Burnsall Green. Almost two centuries after this incident, the same thing happened again in 1991 after the maypole had been repaired and left on the green for the paint to dry. Nobody could ever prove that a suspiciously similar pole erected in Thorpe on May Day was not the very same one.

Take a stroll up the village street to the parish church with its eye-catching midnight blue clock dial. Dating back to the 12th century, the church is reckoned to be the oldest site of Christian worship in the Dales. Indeed, St Wilfred, to whom the parish church is dedicated, is known to have preached the Christian message in AD690 from a boulder in the riverbed. Known as St Wilfred's Pulpit, I can only hazard a guess as to which particular specimen this might refer to. Perhaps some knowledgeable reader can offer enlightenment. In a period when pagan gods were the norm, perhaps Wilfred's choice of stage was a wise decision.

The church's unique appeal is immediately apparent on stepping through the lychgate. Rotating on a central pivot, it is controlled by a weight secreted within the stone gatepost. This unusual entrance is matched only by the antics of a past incumbent. The Revd John Adcott often got the pages of his sermon mixed up and simply read them as they appeared, expecting his congregation to sort them out. On other occasions, he forgot the sermon altogether and merely read excerpts from the bible. Some of his flock preferred this and deliberately hid the sermons.

Wander back down past the Methodist chapel with its petite spire, keeping a watchful eye open for the right of way located on the right. Immediately before the sharp left-hander, a narrow passage gated at either end squeezes between neighbouring cottages. Once in the field behind, the path heads in a north-westerly direction.

After crossing the first stile and adjoining field, we arrive at a walled track that is stiled at both sides. Thereafter count off 6 stiles in rapid succession, which will bring you to a stretch of rising ground where the path leans to the right. Meet the wall ahead and halfway along mount another stile, ten in total since leaving Burnsall.

Stroll over the crest of this grassy shoulder and down to cross Badger Lane. Then stick with the wall in the next field on your right for 100 metres only before bending away to the left and the far side. Cross two more stiles to reach a narrow beck then climb out of this shallow side valley to circle around behind the line of trees ahead. Mount a fence stile and continue onward with a wall on the left to reach a walled track. Amble down this to merge with a back lane heading left into the secluded outpost of Thorpe. No maypole in sight when I passed this way (June 1999) nor does the village appear to have any intention of embracing the new millennium, seemingly content to settle for its unaffected past. Tourism has definitely passed Thorpe by without a trace of regret from the inhabitants.

Safe from marauding brigands in days gone by, it is a mystery in itself as to why the village should have been home to more than its fair share of cobblers and shoemakers. Monks in the surrounding abbeys were frequent customers and it is said that shoes made by the Thorpe cobblers were amongst the finest in the land.

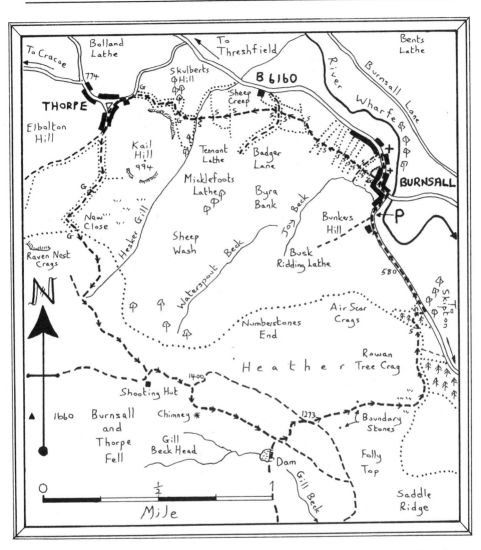

Angling left at the walled triangle of greenery that marks the heart of the village, it becomes clear why the residents of Burnsall overlooked this remote spot in their search for the elusive maypole back in 1804. Nor was there any sign of their newest acquisition, which would appear to have been hidden away to prevent any surreptitious plundering. When the paved road ends take the left of two tracks and accompany this walled corridor up the fellside to its terminus.

Remains of lead smelting on Burnsall Moor

Take a look over to the prominent hill on the right. This is Elbolton Hill, with a cave just below the summit that is reputed to be the haunt of fairies. The name means Elves' Hill and people were convinced that these little creatures held moonlight dances up there. Primitive troglodytes are known to have inhabited the cave and when it was excavated in 1888 twelve skeletons dating back 2000 years were discovered.

One story concerning the fairies of Elbolton involves a man returning to Burnsall along the path below the cave and witnessing one of the nocturnal revels. Keeping quiet so as not to disturb them, he nevertheless was caught up in the fun and called out to them. Frightened at this intrusion, they attacked him, but being tiny beings were only able to nip his legs. He managed to catch one and rushed home intending to surprise his family with this stupendous catch. On reaching into his pocket, he found it was empty and nobody would believe his story. It comes as no surprise to learn that many of these fairy stories were narrated after a visit to the local tavern. An over-indulgence of best bitter is apt to inflame the imagination, especially when a return home passes close to such a place as Elbolton Hill.

A gate gives access to an extensive tract of gritstone moorland covered with heather interspersed with couches of bilberry. Although privately owned and used for the sport of grouse shooting, the public have been granted the right of access. But not, it should be stressed, if accompanied by their canine companions, which one assumes would have a detrimental effect on the breeding habits of the red grouse.

Bear left to follow a thin track along a shallow trench. On reaching a pair of more pronounced gullies, take the one on the left, which will bring you to the substantial cutting carved out by Hesker Gill. Our route slants right, following the upper rim of this severely notched tributary feeding into the mighty Wharfe. At its upper limit, join a more established track heading left across the featureless terrain.

After a quarter of a mile, you should come within 100 metres of the moor wall, thereafter leaning away towards a remote hut. The path merges with a major track close to this stone shooting lodge which is easily reached by shooters using the fell road. On reflection, you would be advised not to venture onto these grouse moors on or about the 'glorious' 12th August when the hunting season begins. I would hate to be the cause of any reader's untimely demise in the name of sport.

Make a left along the track until a break of trail where you should take the right fork, passing close to an old chimney. Continue down the gently shelving gradient until opposite the track branching right across the dammed lip of a small reservoir. Immediately beyond this junction, a track slanting left should be taken. Snaking through the heather like the adders that are known to inhabit these moors, the track joins the one previously abandoned after 200 metres. In spring, you may be fortunate, depending on your viewpoint, to witness these asps mating in a ritual dance.

Lean right for 50 metres, keeping a watch for the indistinct bifurcation on the left. This thin trod ploughs a deep furrow through increasingly dense heather stands so pay heed to hidden boulders as the trail drops down to the wall encompassing the moor. Generally quite easy to follow, it fades in the marshy tract as the wall is neared. Swing left alongside the wall, following it down to the lower group of trees, entered via a stile. Inside the wood, lean immediately left along the wall until it bends away right down through the dense canopy, eventually depositing you on the B6160.

Now head left down the hill into Burnsall and another chance to root out that mystical maypole. One has to wonder if is it only brought out for the annual May Day celebrations.

29. Appletreewick

Simon Says...

Mysteries: Simon's Seat 1590 feet(485m), GR 079598; Trollers Gill, GR 069619; Low Hall, GR 049602

Distance Walked: 8½ miles. Short walk: 4 miles

Total Height Climbed: 1550 feet, 473 metres. Short walk: 1050 feet, 320 metres

Start/Finish: Driving north up the B6160 from Bolton Abbey, turn right at Barden Tower to cross the River Wharfe. Continue along this side road for 1½ miles, until How Beck is crossed where a small pull-in is available at GR 060593. An alternative with more space is to fork right up the Howgill track, parking at GR 065591.

Terrain: Bleak heather moorlands pockmarked with gritstone outcroppings characterise the fell country above the gentle pitch of the serene Wharfe valley. Clear paths all the way.

Nearest Shops: Burnsall

Map Required: Ordnance Survey 1:25000 Outdoor Leisure 2, Yorkshire Dales Southern & Western areas

O ut of sight, out of mind! The old adage aptly describes this circuit that is solely reserved for the discerning walker. And as a route of premier distinction, we could never consider it to be 'out of season'. Always fresh and exhilarating at any time of year, it must surely rank as one of those that are 'out of this world'.

Coniferous plantations fringe the lower slopes, affording a protective scarf for Simon who has seen fit to plonk himself on the highest part of Barden Fell. This high-level plateau is private land to which the public have been granted free access. Being grouse moors, however, there is some restriction during the shooting season.

After parking near to How Beck Bridge, walk up the walled track to its junction with that serving Howgill and Dalehead (located further up the tributary streams feeding into Fir Beck). Cross straight over through a gate to climb the forest trail that squirms up the acclivitous lower slope of Flask Brow like a giant python. Our route keeps right of a prominent bridge to enter the dense canopy of fir and spruce, at which point a steeper short cut can be taken alongside the wall thus chopping off the zigzags. When it straightens out, straddle a stile to accompany the broad concourse up to the heather moors above the confining wall.

Now on 'access land', bear left alongside the wall for 100 metres until an obvious bifurcation laid with creamy white limestone chippings forks right this side of How Beck. The path winds up an easy gradient on to the broad swathe of Barden Fell. Exposed clusters of dark gritstone boulders weathered into sinister formations rise out of the heather like ancient giants sleeping after a night on the town.

More relevant to the modern world and a political hot potato are the numerous ones from which shotgun volleys echo across the moor once the beaters have done their work. The chattering squawk from disturbed grouse is almost humanoid, a ploy no doubt honed to perfection over the years to distract those who would seek their demise.

On reaching a trail junction head north, initially aiming for Truckle Crags. Pass to the right of this rocky oasis and 100 metres beyond, bear left towards the more senior rock theatre with the trig column clearly visible atop Simon's Seat. This chaotic display of oversized boulders requires great care if broken bones are to be avoided – clearly something of a handicap if you are to get the most out of this fine walk.

Make your way across the rock garden to the highest point, where an extensive panorama opens up. Thought to have been a sacred place where Druids practised their pagan rituals at the dawn of time, it later acquired its name from Saint Simon or possibly Sigmund. Infinitely more colourful is the story concerning a shepherd called Simon who found an abandoned baby hidden amongst the cluster of rocks on the summit. Unmarried and ignorant of how to care for a tiny infant, the old man sought the help of other shepherds in the area. All agreed to contribute time and other resources towards the child's welfare. He grew into a strong lad and became known as Simon Amang 'em as a result of his life in what must have been one the earliest communes. He was commemorated by having a lesser pile of stones named after him a half mile to the north-east.

Retrace your steps to the midpoint of the rock theatre where a break enables you to descend a clear path that drops quite steeply through the heather. From here, continue down the north-west flank of the fell where the true severity of the craggy excrescence can be seen in all its majestic glory. The path meanders in a general northerly direction below this startling upsurge of The Seat.

On reaching the intake wall, mount the stile and accompany the zigzagged groove down the steeply shelving cant slicing a path through the bracken. Cross straight over the track contouring this lower section of fellside to slant down to the gate close to Dalehead Farm.

Head left for the return down the access track to the start if your brain has experienced a malfunction informing you that a visit to a well-beloved mother-in-law is required. Otherwise, after 100 metres slip through a gate on the right, cutting back behind a ruined laithe to locate a hidden stile. On the far side of the wall, traverse the field nudging a wall corner to mount a stile then continuing on towards Blands Beck. Over the footbridge, mount the facing bank to sidle between the cottages of High Skyreholme, gated at back and front.

Take a left down the lane, leaning right once the bridge that spans Skyreholme Beck has been crossed. Stroll up the access road serving Parcevall Hall, which remains hidden amongst its circlet of trees. Will Nevison, also known as Swift Nick, was welcomed here as a fugitive seeking refuge from the law and other ne'er-do-wells after the reward posted for his capture (See Walk 21). Using the central bedroom on the first floor, his horse was stabled underneath for a quick getaway should the need for a rapid exit transpire.

Take a left through a gate to follow the beck upstream. After negotiating another gate and stile our route slips by Gill Laithe, climbing gradually above the valley floor. Beyond the next stile the path skirts a line of crags, keeping above the flat bottomland. Now in a deep cutting, interest quickens as we straddle the next stile where two tributary valleys break to left and right.

The main path accompanies the left arm, but for a more sporting alternative fork right round Middle Hill to another wall stile at the entrance to Trollers Gill. This huge rent in the limestone barrier rises sheer on either side, with isolated yews clutching precariously to the creviced scar. Gaunt and forbidding, the stony bed extends for 200 metres, hemming in the ravine and helping to perpetuate the myth of the "Troller Barguest".

Whilst picking a careful route between the rampant forces of this eroded canyon, remember that after heavy rain the beck seethes and ferments as it pours through the narrow fissure. On the day I

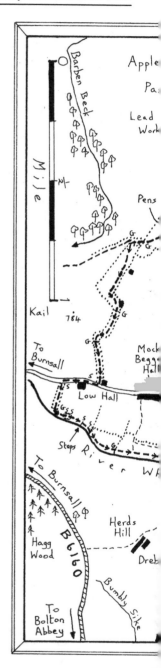

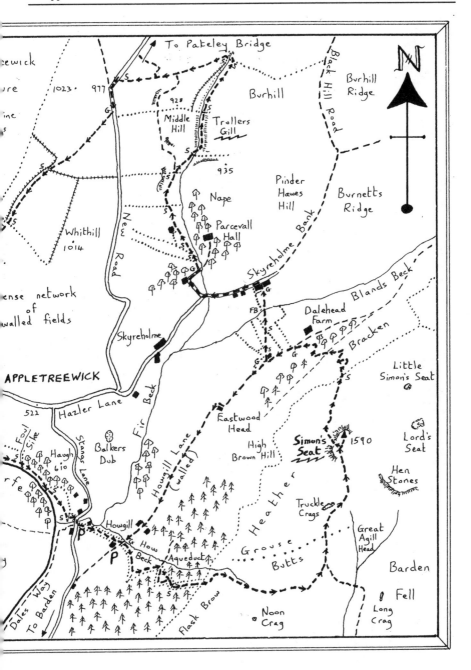

A sinister presence can be felt in the ravine of Trollers Gill

passed this way all was quiet, the beck filtering beneath the rocky duvet. And keep a wary eye on the overhead rim from where trolls have been known to hurl stones onto the exposed pates of those passing below.

Originating from the German for 'mountain demon', this particular barguest resembled a large dog. With bright, staring eyes it roared and capered like a demented banshee. The creature lurked in a cave gouged from the bare limestone, terrifying those who dared to venture into the chasm after dark. The man who gave his name to this awesome crack was foolish enough to think he could best the loathsome creature in its own domain. Entering the ravine on the stroke of midnight, his grisly quest met with a devastating response that left the poor challenger lifeless. A shepherd discovered the body next morning. "And marks were imprest upon the dead man's breast, But they seemed not by mortal hand." The corpse was later buried in the graveyard at Burnsall.

Leaving the confines of Trollers Gill behind, mount a ladder stile over a wall and continue up this more shallow section, keeping to the right bank of Skyreholme Beck. After straddling the next stile, cross the beck and another stile to climb half left up the grassy bank known as Gill Heads. Crest this open fellside and drop down to merge with the original track left behind in the valley bottom. After another 100 metres, leave this clear route to branch left up a thin trod which is made easy to follow by the provision of marker posts all the way to the fell road. Bear left along this, rounding the sharp left-hander and sticking with the road for a further 100 metres until a gate is reached on the right.

Go through it and along a clear fell track that descends the gently shelving swell of Appletreewick Pasture. Now the preserve of wandering woollies, it was once a rich source of lead with many shafts and mine workings. Eventually the track bends right through a gate and down a narrow, walled passage. After 100 metres, leave this major trail to accompany another branching left through a gate. In a series of twists and turns this will bring you out on the road beside the Craven Arms at the western edge of Appletreewick Village (pronounced Aptrick). Boasting an ancient pedigree stretching back to the Dark Ages, the village has thus far effectively resisted the onslaught of tourism.

It was famous in the 19th century for its onion fair, which provided valuable sustenance to the Dales folk. The most important of the annual fairs lasted for three days and all manner of animals were traded on Sheep Fair Hill behind the Craven Arms. Hawkers plied their wares along the main street and all enjoyed a jolly time.

Wherever you go in the region, the name of Craven is a constant reminder of the benefactor who brought prosperity to the Dales. This link stems from High Hall at the eastern end of the village where William Craven was born in 1548. Luck smiled on this 'Dick Whittington of the Dales' who achieved fame and fortune through honesty and hard work. Often returning to walk the fells that he loved, his name became legendary through his philanthropic endeavours.

Turn right past the village stocks outside the Craven Arms and stroll down to the imposing edifice of Low Hall with its enormous stone trough built in 1658 by Thomas Preston. As you pass by, mull over the reason why Preston's ghost was doomed to wander the gloomy corridors of the hall. It would rattle the fittings and shake the rafters, frightening the inhabitants, until it was finally despatched in Dibb Gill, at a spot known as Preston's Well.

Depart this ancient seat by continuing down the road until a walled lane is reached on the left connecting with the riverbank. Mount the stile and gate at the far end then swing left, heading downstream. A short fenced section enclosed by stiles is followed soon after by another enclosed phase where the path climbs a flight of steps above the river. Thereafter, follow the broad river terrace for half a mile until the wooded enclave of Haugh is reached.

·Stride over Foul Sike and through the stile into the tree cover, where the path keeps above the churning torrent of the rapids. Pinched between constricting valley sides, the Wharf is here forced apart by a rocky isle in midstream. Exit from the woods by a stile at the far end, bearing half left away from the river and across flat pastures. Mount a fence stile adjoining the tributary of How Beck and walk onward to squeeze through a gap in the bridge parapet and back to the car pull-in.

No other walk in this collection can surpass this particular offering for the variety of terrain and scenery visited. Grim heather moorland surrenders to wooded pastures hiding dark secrets and then to a scintillating ravine. Not quite akin to the sizeable proportions of Gordale Scar, but definitely one to be included on a list of must-dos. Add the visit to the intoxicating village of Aptrick, and this walk possesses all the hallmarks of a classic.

30. Bolton Abbey
Striding down Wharfedale

Mysteries: Bolton Priory, GR 074542; The Strid, GR 063565

Distance Walked: 7½ miles

Total Height Climbed: 700 feet, 213 metres

Start/Finish: Make use of the official car park in the village of Bolton Abbey by forking right off the B6160 at the Cavendish Memorial and taking the access road down to the riverside recreation area. Should this be full, continue up the road towards Burnsall for a further quarter mile where a broad pull-in is available on the right.

Terrain: The spacious open fields above the Wharfe valley contrast with the popular wooded thoroughfare along the riverbank between The Strid and Bolton Abbey.

Nearest Shop: Bolton Abbey

Map Required: Ordnance Survey 1:25000 Outdoor Leisure 2, Yorkshire Dales Southern & Western areas

Built on property now owned by the Duke of Devonshire stands the magnificent edifice of Bolton Priory. Not to be confused with Bolton Castle in Wensleydale (See Walk 11), nor even Bolton Abbey the actual village where the priory stands, this part of Wharfedale attracts visitors all year round. But thankfully, this is only along the established footways that line both sides of the river between Bolton Abbey and The Strid. Few people have eyes for the heights above which offer first-class walking terrain for those who enjoy the solitude of the fells. Approaching from the direction of the A59, a reminder of the area's aristocratic landlord appears almost immediately in the name of the local hotel.

Soon after the stone buildings of Bolton Abbey remind us that these were once outbuildings of the priory, the largest being the 14th-century gatehouse later converted to a shooting lodge used by the Duke of Devonshire. An archway over the road was an aqueduct conveying water to drive the priory mill wheel.

Never more than a small centre of ecclesiastical endeavour, the Augustinians, who were known as 'black canons' on account of their dark habits, ran Bolton Priory. They were practical and more outgoing than other monastic orders, "The Augustine Rule is more courteous than that of Benedict. Among them one is well shod, well clothed, and well fed. They go out when they like, mix with the world, and talk at table." Happy, fun-loving trendy types of 12th-century society it would seem. Is this where the allusion to dark habits really stems from?

As a priory, it finally went out of business in 1538 when Prior Richard Moone surrendered his charge to the officers of Henry VIII. Like many other similar establishments, Bolton Priory was ravished by the agents of Dissolution, but thankfully the Nave remained intact to become the parish church of St Mary and St Cuthbert.

The ghost of Prior Moone is said to haunt the ruined shell, doubtless awaiting the completion of the west tower first commissioned in 1520. He had to wait almost half a millennium before the ambitious project achieved fruition after an appeal was launched in 1980. Not quite the soaring structure Moone had envisaged, but nonetheless, a welcome finale to a building that witnessed its inception way back in 1120 at Embsay.

This was the most enigmatic phase in the Priory's lengthy history. Legend purports that the first building was erected under the benefaction of Cecilia de Romille, although it is to her daughter Alice that we must now turn our attention for it was she who bore a son at Egremont Castle. The boy became heir to vast estates in Cumbria and Yorkshire and was tutored in management skills by his mother so as to further the prosperity of his inheritance. Known as The Boy of Egremont, it was during one particular fateful visit to Bolton Abbey that he and his faithful hound went hunting in the woods adjoining the River Wharfe. Arriving at the awesome cleft known as The Strid, the pair halted. Even then it must have presented an exhilarating dare for a young lad. Tons of fermenting water bursting through gaps in the gritstone bedrock had carved out a spectacular fissure in the leafy glade.

And like many others before and since, the boy accepted the challenge to leap the chasm. As he made the jump, the nervous dog hung back, indeci-

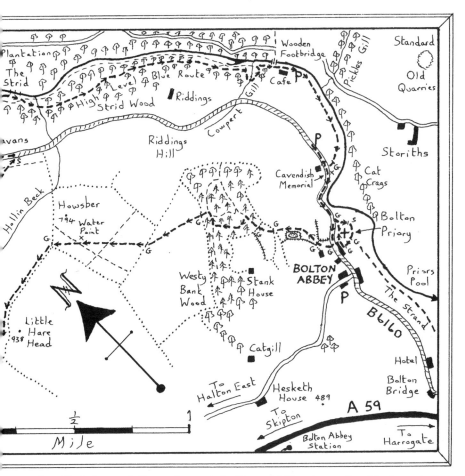

sion that dragged them down into the whirling torrent with devastating consequences. Both were drowned. Distraught with grief at the loss of her son, Alice was determined to preserve his memory. She persuaded the Augustinians to move from Embsay to the more sheltered location beside the Wharfe. With financial assistance, the new priory began to take shape around 1154 and flourished until the mid-14th century, when Scots raiders burnt it to the ground. Later rebuilt by Richard Moone, he could not have foreseen the winds of change that were soon to sweep aside the established church.

To visit the priory and its environs, walk down the road past the Cavendish Memorial until the entrance to the church is reached. This local dignitary is commemorated in numerous pubs and street names in the area and was the Secretary to Ireland in 1882. Unfortunately, Mr Cavendish was unable to achieve much, his life being violently cut short by a republican group known as The Invincibles. This memorial was erected in 1886.

Go through the gate and almost immediately bear left through another gate and along the path that circles round the graveyard, supposedly the final resting place of the Norton Family from Rylstone (See Walk 27). The attraction of such a setting for the priory is obvious, in spite of the floods that invaded the grounds from time to time. Keep right to make a complete circuit of priory and attendant church and pass through two more gates to gain the front access track. Passing the glass-fronted entrance to the west tower, return to the B6160 and head left for 150 metres then take the gated bridleway on the right signposted to Rylstone.

Lean in towards a fence on the right to pass through a gate, then bear half left, keeping right of a fenced pond. The indistinct trail aims for woods ahead, first passing through a wall gate then going onward to the next gate – giving access to the enclosed recess of Westy Bank Wood. Various tracks scythe through the sylvan tract, the official right of way swinging left at the first junction after 100 metres. Circling right, it then bears right at a T-junction and left up to a gate at the edge of the wood.

Carry on across the open grass field, aiming for the left of two prominent hillocks. This will bring you to a gate in the wall at the far side. Now bearing north-west, the improving path passes close to Howsber on the right. Just beyond a water testing point, cross a field track then continue on to the wall corner and another gate.

Swing left alongside the wall on your left behind Little Hare Head until the clear path veers away to the right and up on to the domed knoll of Middle Hare Head, which offers an expansive vista across the gently rolling terrain of Lower Wharfedale. Now drop down off the western shoulder of this rather innocuous mound, accompanying the clear trail through heather to a wall. Beyond the gate, heave right down a path that cuts an obvious route through the bracken to arrive at the fell road 100 metres below a circular airshaft used in the mines. Another 100 metres further down, a gate marks the start of a path heading east alongside the wall. After mounting a wall stile, the thin trod forks left across the lower grass slopes of Stank to brush a wall corner.

Forging onward through a stook of reeds, it wanders right alongside the intake wall, following it round to the left as it dips towards the valley. When the wall breaks left down to the road, keep straight on and make a slanted descent to gain the road through a stile. Turn left for 300 metres and past a caravan site before leaning right into Strid car park. Keep striding ahead along a clear track through the woods to reach the riverbank of the Wharfe, ignoring any turnings off this major footway. Bend right to accompany the river downstream at this higher level until a narrower, stonier alternative presents itself, forking left. Drop down into open woodland where The Strid can be experienced in all its fearsome glory.

Truly this is a majestic setting for such a perilous feature. Many have attempted what appears to be a simple leap across the narrow cleft, too late realising their folly and succumbing to the ultimate penalty.

Resist the temptation to leap across The Strid

Do not be one of those foolhardy poltroons who ignore the bright red warning signs. A white horse is supposed to rise from the bubbling spume each time The Strid claims another victim.

Wordsworth recognised the unique allure of this enchanting locale in his customary format thus:

This striding place is called the Strid
A name it took of yore;
A thousand years hath it born that name,
And shall a thousand more.

He went on to tell how a young man came to leap across the chasm but failed due to the timidity of his dog, and so

The boy is in the arms of Wharf,
And strangled by a merciless force;
For never more was young Romilly seen
Till he rose a lifeless corpse.

A little way past The Strid, an open glade is reached providing information about this special place together with aspects associated with the region's natural history. Strike uphill from here to accompany the 'blue route' if you prefer a quieter alternative to the well-populated riverside walk. Pursuing a thin trail that winds through the upper limit of Strid Wood, it eventually circumvents the side valley of Cowpert Gill to make a zig-zag return to the lower track at the edge of the woods.

Stroll on past the Cavendish Pavilion which offers ease and refreshment together with a huge car park. Stick to the grass verge beside the river before striking out across the flat grassy plain of Sand Holme. At the far side, a flight of steps with a gate at the top will return you to the Cavendish Memorial; the end of a walk where the blurred edge of reality has on more than one occasion been made crystal clear with tragic consequences.

More Mysteries!

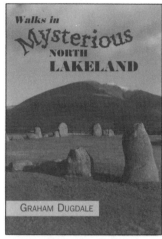

WALKS IN MYSTERIOUS LANCASHIRE
Graham Dugdale
£6.95

WALKS IN MYSTERIOUS NORTH LAKELAND
Graham Dugdale
£6.95

WALKS IN MYSTERIOUS SOUTH LAKELAND
Graham Dugdale
£6.95

WALKS IN MYSTERIOUS NORTHAMPTONSHIRE
Marian Pipe & Mia Butler
£6.95

WALKS IN MYSTERIOUS OXFORDSHIRE
Laurence Main
£6.95

WALKS IN MYSTERIOUS DEVON
Laurence Main
£6.95

WALKS IN MYSTERIOUS SOMERSET
Laurence Main
£6.95

WALKS IN MYSTERIOUS WILTSHIRE
Laurence Main
£6.95

WALKS IN MYSTERIOUS WALES
Laurence Main
£6.95